CHEERS FOR
THE GROWING SEASON...

Thought provoking, sincere and approachable. I highly recommend this book for anyone looking to delve deeper into the possible reason why humans have been obsessed with wine for thousands of years. Nelson takes the reader on a journey through the parallels of wine and the human soul. He creates a safe space around two complex topics and guides the reader into deeply thinking about how appreciating wines could lead us to live a more worldly spiritual life, like Jesus did. Great read!

> — Jaclyn Misch, *DipWSET Candidate, Masters in Wine Management, research team, Karen MacNeil's "The Wine Bible", wine educator, Napa Valley Wine Academy*

The Growing Season arrests you—Pay attention! Attend!—for there is a world of magic all around. It is always there, but you have to get your feet dirty to see it, find it, taste it. This book follows Nelson's journey, one we take with him, into cultivating a deeper, more attentive love of wine and of Jesus.

> — Christopher Mark, *founder and President of Vintality, a viticulture company that uses technology to uncover and reveal terroir in all its forms*

Through the imagery and process of grape becoming wine, Boschman invites us to see our spiritual journeys as rooted in the cycles of life and the rhythms of the earth. Found in the humble and accessible day-to-day moments of our lives, our handiwork, our interactions with others, and the experience of our senses, he invites us to see that there is nowhere else we need to be to encounter ourselves, each other, and our Creator.

—Hillary L. McBride, *PhD, Psychologist, Author, Podcaster*

As a foot-crushed grape still in spiritual fermentation, I find that Boschman's/Jesus's wine-soul imagery resonates deeply. Nelson is a wise friend and experienced vintner who creatively guides faith shifts like mine. He clarified my own long process as a Welch's™ grape Baptist into the deep dessert reds of the Orthodox chalice, all with a smile on stained and satisfied lips. A delightful read!

— Bradley Jersak, *Dean of Theology & Culture, St. Stephen's University, author of A* More Christlike God

Nelson Boschman's *The Growing Season*, like some wines, masks its strength by a deceptive smoothness. I felt, from beginning to end, like I was being guided through a tasting by a knowledgeable friend. But at the end I realized I had more than tasted: I had savoured a full bottle of wisdom about what it takes to make both a fine wine—and a fine soul. "Wine makes the heart glad," says the Psalmist. And so does this book.

— Dr. Loren Wilkinson, *professor emeritus of philosophy and interdisciplinary studies, Regent College (Vancouver, BC, Canada).*

The Growing Season is a wine guide that is also part memoir and spiritual journal; or to put it another way, it is a tender pastoral letter with excellent advice on wine. Nelson Boschman's first book is a demonstration of and invitation to "tending the truth contained within" using creative analogies on the transformation from grape to wine. You will encounter music, centering prayer, biodiversity, preservatives, poetry, and rich imagery. This book is a narrative journey with a bouquet of flavours which is both invigorating and enriching.

— Janet E. Boldt, *MA Intercultural Studies. MA Theology. Owner of Madrona Mentoring and Soul Care. Professor Emerita, Columbia Bible College.*

Reading *The Growing Season* was not only informative (I learned so much!), but it inspired me to contemplate the gifts of this world through a new lens. Wine is one of those gifts, but in Nelson Boschman's playful and imaginative text, he also invites us to consider the earth, and our fellow humans, with deep appreciation and love. The Growing Season begins with wine, but the book sets down deeper roots, taking the reader through the vineyard and on a spiritual journey.

— Kaitlin Williams, *Artistic Director, Pacific Theatre (Vancouver, BC, Canada)*

This book will do more than encourage you to reach for a glass with friends. It will encourage you to "make friends with mystery." Biblical faith would be unrecognizable without its love for wine. Nelson Boschman's book will show you why.

— Jason Byassee, *Butler Chair in Homiletics and Biblical Hermeneutics, Vancouver School of Theology, long-time contributor to The Christian Century*

This book is not just information. It's a study. It's not only about interest. It's personal stories of vulnerability, blended with history and viticulture. This is a book about taking time to reflect, to linger, to marinade until one is changed. It's about hope and healing. It's about intimacy—with each and every little moment and thing—and the sparkle this brings to all of life. This book is about prose. Its cadence waltzes the reader into the rhythm of Nelson's life and heart. *The Growing Season* is a deep look within, an outward glance, and a movement into all that matters most.

— Lorie Martin, *associate director of the Centre for Spiritual Renewal (Langley, BC, Canada), board member of The Contemplative Society (Cynthia Bourgeault)*

Throughout this detailed and fascinating story of how grapes are grown and wine is made, Nelson serves as an unpretentious sommelier of the spirit, refining our palates to appreciate the intricacies not only of wine-making but of spiritual formation— how our hearts are grown, cultivated, and brought to maturity by the attentive and loving hand of the Master vintner—and the ways we can participate as apprentices in that soulful work. Guided by the author's enthusiasm for all three of his subjects— fine wines, human souls, and God's work in us—we are tutored in the art of tasting and seeing their goodness. The book's great achievement is the recognition that winemaking is more than just a metaphor for spiritual growth; the two processes are intricately and intimately linked, both of them rooted in the terroir of God's kingdom, lovingly nurtured by the same Divine hand. Could it be that God delights in us and our growing as much as Nelson does in a glass of Pinot Noir? A book to savour!

— Ron Reed, *actor, writer, director, founder and Artistic Director Emeritus of Vancouver's Pacific Theatre, graduate of Regent College and the California Institute of the Arts*

I loved this book! *The Growing Season* is a full-on sensory adventure, grounded in the earthy slowness of wine-making and soul-ripening. Nelson Boschman is a generous companion on both those journeys, a trustworthy steward of wine and life.

— Deb Arndt, *BA, BEd, facilitator, spiritual director,*
Executive Director of SoulStream

The Growing Season is a delicious read. I suggest savouring it slowly. Chapter by chapter, Nelson brings us a very earthy yet mysterious spirituality as he reflects on winemaking and the journey of our souls.

— Steve Klassen, *MA in New Testament Studies,*
Director of the MARK Centre (Abbotsford, BC, Canada)

Reading this first book by Boschman brought me such a profound and playful mix of joy, pleasure and insight. I felt like I was in a tasting room the whole time I was reading the book, each chapter hosting me gently, taking my hand from dirt to glass, from Spring to Winter, from soil to soul. You are in for a sumptuous, earthy, spiritual treat that will enrich your life on all levels.

— Brent Unrau, *MAC, RCC, counsellor, spiritual director,*
husband/father/grandfather, practitioner of intentional
community at Kingfisher Farm (South Surrey, BC, Canada)

Nelson has written a delicious book about caring for your soul while being deeply engaged with other humans, all embedded in an entertaining wine-appreciation primer. These elements are so vulnerably blended within Nelson-as-a-fine-wine-in-progress, you cannot help but become friends with him as you read. As well as learning about: (1) how to pronounce terroir; (2) how grape farming inspires growing a church slowly; (3) how to negotiate the dangerous business of being human; (4) the fun of embracing a Nap Ministry; and (5) how flourishing as a person is rooted in curiosity. There is only one way now to satisfy YOUR curiosity about these topics. Skip further sipping and buy the whole bottle, er, book!

— Dan Williams, *church planter in wine country*

Like a vineyard manager with their vines, Boschman invites readers to join him in self-reflection that is marked by patience and tenderness. By telling the story of wine creation in connection to faith, he emphasizes our sensory experiences as seekers who undergo seasons of doubt, challenge, and renewal in visceral ways.

— Aubrianna Pennington, *MA Theological Studies, Wine and Spirits Retail Associate*

THE GROWING SEASON
Contemplations on Wine and the Soul

FIRST PAPERBACK EDITION PUBLISHED IN 2022
Library of Congress Cataloging-in-Publication
Data is available upon request.

Cover & Interior Design: Chelsea McKenzie

ISBN: 978-1-7780831-0-5

To Terri & Adriana —
so glad we get to grow together

Contents

Foreword

My husband Dave and I met Nelson when he was a worship arts professor at Columbia Bible College. Dave and I had just started dating, and I remember him raving about a class that explored the theology found in "secular" film, art, and music. Who wouldn't want to enroll in a class where you got to study Rembrandt and watch The Shawshank Redemption?

I don't think Nelson knew this at the time, but before they immigrated to Canada from South Korea, Dave's family ran a local video shop. He spent many of his formative years rewinding VHS tapes for 10 won (about a penny) per video. Dave's father would come back from business trips and give him the latest CD by Michael Jackson. Music and film were integral parts of Dave's upbringing, closely connected to memories of his father.

When Dave was thirteen, he immigrated to Canada, where his entire family converted to Christianity. Soon after, his father died after a year-long battle with cancer. Dave's youth group years were filled with faith-fuelled passion, like many '90s church experiences were. He led musical worship with on-fire-for-Jesus gusto and burned all his CDs that weren't CCM (contemporary Christian music) with heartfelt penitence. All that fervour led Dave to study worship arts at Columbia Bible College.

That's where Nelson and several other professors introduced him to a novel idea that contradicted much of his early experience in the church. Namely, that a redemptive quality can be found in what is often deemed "worldly". We just need to learn to look closer. Seeing ways that faith, film, and music can intersect left a big impression on Dave's developing mind and grieving heart. It helped him reconcile his childhood experiences of film and music, experiences shared with his father, to the redemptive presence of Christ in the everyday.

I've been witness to Dave and Nelson's respective journeys, which have been both separate and parallel. Student and professor became friends. They both became parents. They performed jazz or folk music in and outside the church. They blended ministry, work, and family life with trips to film and music conferences, or to wine country.

Fast-forward two decades later: Dave is making wine and Nelson is writing about it.

As you read, you'll quickly see that Nelson makes his purpose very clear. This is not a theology book and it is not a wine book. It is, rather, a book that guides you to see the redemptive qualities in what you (if you're a person of faith) may have grown up thinking was off-limits.

In some ways, it almost seems inevitable that Nelson and Dave's journeys led them to wine. A musician is already one who is sensitive to the auditory pleasures. It makes sense that a musician would also be drawn to olfactory and visceral pleasures.

Nelson's story, Dave's story, and all our stories remind me of a scene Nelson paints in an early chapter, where cutworms invade the vineyard and wild mustard is planted to restore balance. In a vineyard, not everything is black and white. There are harmful and beneficial pests, and harmful and beneficial weeds. "Everything is permissible but not everything is beneficial." It takes a skillful vine grower to see a threat and understand its effects on the entire ecosystem.

You don't have to be a theologian or a wine connoisseur to relate to this book. Just learn how to look, really look, and you may encounter the Divine in your next glass.

LOIS CHO
CEO and founder of CHO Wines

Dave and Lois Cho are a husband and wife duo making wine in Willamette Valley, Oregon with a focus on high elevation Pinot Noir and sparkling wine. They launched their winery during the pandemic, purchased 77 acres in the Chehalem Mountains AVA, and will begin the arduous journey of establishing a vineyard and tasting room in 2023, while raising their three children.

A Taster

What happens when your closest friends move to the Wine Capital of Canada?

You visit. You make multiple visits. You tour wineries. Over time you realize that tasting wine with friends is one of your favourite activities—like, ever. And eventually, it dawns on you that a new passion is bursting to life.

What happens when you're a pastor and you have a sabbatical coming up?

You reflect. You read. You pray. You listen. You pay attention. To what you need, and need to do, make, or create. Then, one morning, an idea that might carry a spark of Divine Imagination comes to you: to write a book that explores what winemaking and soul formation might have in common.

This is my story. This book was first planted in the soil of my soul.

I am not a wine expert or a certified sommelier. I'm a pastor, a spiritual director, and a wine enthusiast who spent a month of my first sabbatical learning about wine and apprenticing in the Okanagan Valley (British Columbia, Canada). Then, I spent a month visiting Bordeaux, France, one of the world's most famous and important wine regions.

Though not (yet?) an expert, I continue to learn about wine through reading, listening, tasting, and both formal and casual study. I have earned my Wine & Spirit

Education Trust (WSET) Level 1 training. This book has been reviewed and fact-checked by winemakers, certified sommeliers, and other industry professionals who know more than I do. If you're a wine expert, I want you to be part of this conversation, and I realize that to enter it, it's important you're not distracted or turned off by incorrect information.

I am also not an expert theologian. I do hold a master's degree from a reputable seminary. But more importantly, I am someone who seeks to apprentice myself to the way of Jesus in every aspect of my life. I'm a ministry practitioner committed to the local church and driven by an impulse to live relationally and creatively. I am hardwired to make connections between the created order and the inner workings of the human soul.

So. This is not a book about wine or winemaking. Nor is it a book on the theology or spirituality of wine. (Vast volumes have, of course, been written by experts on these topics. I will introduce you to a few that have inspired me along the way and made my book better.)

What do we have here then? This book explores the inter-section between vineyard, cellar, tasting room, and soul. I believe a closer look at the transformation that occurs from grape to glass could lend much to the conversation about what it means to flourish as a human being.

I hope you'll agree.

Welcome to *The Growing Season*.

Consider the Lilies

Who could have been more invested in physical life on earth than Jesus? I've been preaching lately on "consider the lilies of the field." The way he could look around and see anything and make it part of what he was talking about.

—Barbara Brown Taylor

By taking a long and thoughtful look at what God has created, people have always been able to see what their eyes as such can't see...

—Romans 1:20, *The Message*

I've been searching for a more this-worldly spirituality.

Something not so fixated on questions of where we go when we die.
Something more inclined to explore what it means to live well, to
flourish as humans, here and now.
Something a little less pearly gates and a lot more consider the lilies.

I've been searching for a good while. I've met obstacles and
challenges. For one thing, I'm a pastor, and as it turns out, many
church folk are fairly focused on the next world.

I'm also a musician and I've led musical worship in church for
years. One time, I got some feedback I didn't expect and will
never forget.

The sermon was about an ancient Israelite king acting in a way
that was consistent with God's intent: rebuilding Jerusalem, re-
storing city walls, looking after the poor. I wanted our worship
that morning to reflect God's clear concern for the here and now.
I felt energized by these physical, earthy, this-world themes. (You
know, because of my ongoing search.) In preparation, I went to
the Psalms. In this ancient prayer book, rocks and trees, fowl and
fish, streams and stars are all handiwork of the Divine, elements
of a world God loves and invites humans to care for.[1] Because
creation matters deeply, we also find poetic prayers about what it
means to govern with justice and mercy in the Psalms.[2]

For worship that morning, I chose songs that echoed that same
language. Songs that were both this-worldly and centred on
Scripture. They spoke of God as the God of the broken, the friend
of the weak. The God who lifts the needy from the ashes and heals
the barren.

In my mind, it was one of the most down-to-earth worship sets
I'd ever put together. The congregation seemed super into it. They

sang loudly, with lifted hands and hearts ablaze.

As soon as I sat down after the last song, a kind, older woman sitting in the row behind me tapped my shoulder. I turned around. She leaned in close and whispered,

"When you lead worship, you lead us right up to the gates of heaven."

You have got to be kidding, I thought. I'm putting down city-building and justice and she's picking up fluffy clouds and cream cheese.

"Thank you," I said quietly and turned back around.

She meant well. I received it as a compliment. Musical worship ought to give rise to a sense of the transcendent. I'm glad those songs helped that woman feel something Beyond. But at that moment, I cared more about the Immanent.

There's a healthy tension here, of course. All of it matters. Unseen and seen. Spirit and body. Heaven and earth. But, to me, things seemed out of balance.

The spirituality I've been searching for invites me to notice what Jesus noticed. Lilies and sparrows. Sheep and shepherds. Vines and branches. He always seemed to call folks' attention to the concrete. To the material. To things people can see, in order to evoke a different kind of seeing.

Jesus' spirituality was next-level earthy. It was also radically inclusive. In one breath, he's telling us that God cares about birds. In the next, he's saying, "God loves humans even more." People who wrote the earliest accounts of Jesus' life said he was never without a story.[3] He wanted those he encountered to see themselves, to see their own lived experience, in what he said and taught. There was room for everyone in his stories, including those society excluded. And he made it a regular practice to call out anyone who claimed otherwise.[4]

Like so many others, I'm becoming more and more captivated by what Jesus embodied most clearly: a spirituality for the rest of us.

I've been searching for a more this-worldly spirituality.

And like a gravitational pull, there's been a growing sense that it's been searching for me.

In many ways, this book is a chronicling of that search. One that has only intensified over the years. One that led me to spend my sabbatical in more agrarian settings than I usually inhabit.

One that deepened my interest in wine.

I'm curious about your interest in wine, too. Here's one question I'd love to know your answer to: What comes to mind when you think of the wine industry?

A highbrow hobby for rich people?
Pretense and condescension?
An elitist tribe that caters only to the insiders?

To some, the wine industry equals wine snobbery.

In my experience, I've seen very little elitism. Most winefolk I've met are not only professionals but enthusiasts. They're amateurs in the original (French) sense of the word: those who love. They're fanatical about wine and everything to do with it: soil and seasons, vineyards and varietals, cellaring and celebrating. They're passionate about their role in growing grapes, making wine, and helping others appreciate it. And they're quite happy to share their knowledge with anyone willing to listen and learn. Wine snobs do exist, of course. Those who appoint themselves as presiders over a world where, if you have the right credentials, if you know the right people, and if you drink the right wines, you belong. And if you don't, you may as well steer clear.

Yet, another sort of movement is cropping up. A growing group of enthusiasts and professionals are hosting a different kind of conversation. One where everyone is invited.

A good example is the Wine For Normal People podcast, a "wide-ranging but easygoing discussion of wine issues for non-experts."[5] Most new episodes begin with host Elizabeth Schneider saying something like, "Thanks for downloading Wine for Normal People Radio, the podcast for people who like wine but not the snobbery that comes with it." Schneider's tone, manner, and humour set me at ease right away. I felt like I belonged in the conversation. And while the vibe is accessible, it's clear she knows what she's talking about. In fact, Schneider has now written a book by the same title as the podcast. Whether you're just beginning to learn about wine or know a little but want to take a deeper dive, she's a good companion for all of that.

Another is the book, The New Wine Rules by acclaimed wine writer Jon Bonne. On the back cover, Bonne says, "There are few greater pleasures in life than enjoying a wonderful glass of wine. So why does finding and choosing one you like seem so stressful? Now, becoming a happier, more confident wine drinker is easy. The first step is to forget all the needlessly complicated stuff the "experts" have been telling you."[6] The New Wine Rules helps you sort through what can feel like an overwhelming amount of insider info and language when it comes to wine. And how to prioritize your time and attention, not to mention budget. Jon Bonne is like the Rick Steeves of the wine world.

My friend and certified sommelier, Ashley West, is another good example of someone who makes wine appreciation more enjoyable and accessible. She describes her business, Somm at Home, as "an unpretentious approach to wine tasting, events and education in the heart of the Fraser Valley."[7] West has designed a beautiful, straightforward process to discover, taste, and learn about BC wines from the comfort of your home. If you live in the Lower Mainland of British Columbia, Somm at Home is worth checking out.

Unpretentious. Uncomplicated. Wine delight for the rest of us.

Like the wine industry, many books about spirituality and matters of the soul can also make people feel like outsiders. Unless you read certain authors, believe certain things, and use a certain vocabulary, you have nothing to add to the dialogue.

You have picked up a book on wine and the human soul. Two topics that each have significant potential to make you, the reader, feel like you don't belong. You're only a few pages in so far, and I'd love for you to make it to the end. So I thought I'd spend part of the Introduction trying to set your mind at ease.

Here's how I want this book to feel: I want to invite you to this conversation like my friend Paul invites people to play disc golf.

Paul is the best disc golf player I know. He enters tournaments. He even designed a municipal disc golf course. But by his own admission, he's a small fish in a big pond when it comes to his ability. And still, Paul is the closest thing I may ever know to an expert. So when an opportunity arose to play my first round ever, with Disc Golf Paul of all people, I was immediately intimidated.

I began to think of what my drives (aka tee shots) would look like compared to his. I feared what his more experienced friends would think of a neophyte joining their foursome. I envisioned shot after crappy shot drifting into the towering, impenetrable blackberry bushes that hovered around the edges of seemingly every fairway. (That only happened once. And since I was fortunate enough to be playing with another buddy who eats thorny, brambly blackberry bushes for breakfast, my woefully errant shot was retrieved.)

But before these worrisome thoughts could take root, Paul's gift for enthusiastic education and radical inclusion helped me set them aside.

"Boschman! Are you coming to play?"
"Yeah, I've never really played before though."
"Who cares. You will absolutely love it.
        Do you have your own discs?"
"I think I can get a couple."
"Great. I've got a whole bunch you can borrow
        if you need them."

When we got out to the course, Paul greeted me with a huge smile, a massive hug, and a loud, enthusiastic voice that made me feel he was beside himself at the chance to shoot some discs with me.

Even though I was keenly aware of my newbie status as a disc golfer, Paul made me feel like I belonged. Like I mattered. That this eighteen-hole excursion was a safe space to learn, grow, and fling a disc or two into the blackberries.

I want you to feel that same safety as you journey through this book.

I am truly honoured you're here.

Let me say just a bit more about where we're going.

We're here to talk about wine and the soul. Wine, as we all know, doesn't begin as wine. It starts as something different: a grape. It only becomes wine because it goes through a wide-ranging transformative process. Our souls—our inner beings, the essence of who we are—undergo a similar journey. We're going to explore both. One in dialogue with the other.

You and I, you and you, you and God.

I've said this isn't a book about wine. But that's not totally true. I still want you to learn a few wine things. And since we're talking about transformation and change, we're going to follow the wine-making process in chronological order:

Soil
Vineyard
Harvest
Cellar
Bottle

In short, we're going from dirt to glass.

At the same time, we know that the inward soul journey is not always a neat, linear process. Nor is the winemaking journey at times, come to think of it. So we'll allow for detours, side roads, and pit stops along the way.

An earthy, this-worldly spirituality.

That's been my search. And I can't shake the fact that it's also been searching for me. Something has led you to pick up this book.

So I wonder, dear reader:

Is it searching for you too?

SOIL

CHAPTER ONE

Somewhereness

Great wine can only result when the grape

variety is tuned in, like the signal on a radio dial,

to the "channel" of its terroir.

—Karen MacNeil, *The Wine Bible*

Listen to your life. See it for the fathomless mystery it is. In the

boredom and pain of it, no less than in the excitement and

gladness: touch, taste, smell your way to the holy and hidden

heart of it, because in the last analysis all moments are key

moments, and life itself is grace.

—Frederick Buechner, *Now and Then: A Memoir of Vocation*

I wanted to get my hands dirty. I wanted to learn about wine, not by clicking links and turning pages, but by getting out of the office and into the land. I wanted to follow the same journey wine takes from soil to glass. I wanted an immersive experience. A deep dive. And the moment had finally arrived.

In May 2018, after eighteen months of dreaming and planning my first-ever sabbatical, I began my month at Nk'Mip Cellars (pronounced in-ka-meep). Nk'Mip is North America's first Indigenous winery, located in Osoyoos, in British Columbia's Okanagan Valley.

When the idea of a month-long wine apprenticeship first occurred to me, my friend Richard Jones was my first point of contact. Richard is now retired, but he enjoyed a long career in the Canadian wine world. From 1995 to 2006, he was Chief Financial Officer of Vincor International Inc., which eventually became Arterra Wines Canada. Among its many other brands, Arterra owns part of Nk'Mip Cellars. Through Richard's networks, I connected with Arterra, and through them, to Nk'Mip.

It took some time and effort, but eventually, I met the amazing people who were willing and able to provide such a short, intensive, unique experience as a month-long unpaid wine apprenticeship.Beginning with Richard, every person I talked to inevitably asked about who I am and why I wanted to do this.

What makes you want to learn about wine?
What are you hoping to get out of this?
Where are you from again?

These were questions about context, identity, background, and motivation. People I hoped to learn from obviously wanted to make sure I was serious and committed. That I wasn't going to flake out in some way or waste their time and energy.

But some of them were also curious. They wanted to know my story.

Welcome to Nk'mip Cellars. Where are you from?

As part of my apprenticeship, I spent a few days exploring the hospitality side of the industry: the other side of the tasting room counter. On the morning of my first shift, I felt that familiar pairing of nervousness and excitement. I met several of the staff, formally known as tasting room associates, and they all seemed friendly. But who else would I meet? Who would come in to taste that day? Who would I get to serve?

I put on my official Nk'Mip shirt—a charcoal grey, loose-fitting short-sleeve button-down—and a little magnetic badge that linked my name with Nk'Mip's. I made myself a good coffee and ate some cereal. Then, I headed down to my car for the 10-minute drive over from the resort where I was staying, thoughts still racing.

Tasting Room People always seemed to know everything about the wines they were pouring. I was about to become a Tasting Room Person, and I did not know everything about these wines. I knew I needed to say *something*, though. I couldn't just stand there. What did I need to know? As a taster, I always ask questions. Would people ask me questions? What if I didn't know the answers? Would one of my associates help me out, or was I on my own? Was there a cheat sheet?

I got there a bit early for a brief orientation. Before that, I took a minute to drink in the incredible beauty of the tasting room itself. If you've been to Nk'Mip before, you know what I'm talking about. It's a large, open space with high ceilings and tasteful decor influenced by Indigenous art and design, with beautiful stone and tile work on the floors and walls. Expansive windows offer views of the vineyards that surround the winery, as well as Osoyoos Lake below. Whenever I'm in that room, an air of mystery encircles me. I feel both transported and more deeply rooted at the same time.

I looked outside and took a few deep breaths.

Then, I headed over to the other side of the counter to meet Troy Ravndahl, Estate Manager at Nk'Mip. As we pulled bottles out of the fridge, he walked me through the paces:

> How to handle the stemware, including washing, drying, and polishing. (Those glasses gotta sparkle and shine!)
>
> How to explain the various tasting options and what they cost.
>
> Which bottles to use first.
>
> Where to get new bottles when they run out.
>
> How to open the new bottles.
>
> Where to find the information about each of our wines. (There was a cheat sheet! Cue the heavy sigh of relief.)
>
> Which associate would ring up the sales once the tasting was over. (I wasn't there long enough to get trained on the till.)
>
> Where to find empty boxes if people wanted to take home several bottles.

My nerves calmed a bit after the orientation. It helps to get a sense of your bearings in new spaces. *You can do this*, I thought. *You know where you are*, and you're not alone. Soon my fellow associates arrived. Zrinka, Janice, and Deb are lovely humans. They made me feel at home, despite my newness, and were a ton of fun to work with.

There's one more vital bit of training I need to mention. Even before offering the first pour, I was encouraged to ask people a bit about themselves—where they were from, whether they had tasted here before, which wines they enjoy.

This isn't a revolutionary idea, of course. It's Customer Service 101: how to make a good first impression. A courteous attempt to build connection—to show someone they matter as a person, not only as a customer. I took this bit of training to heart, in part because I wanted to be seen in a certain way: as gracious and hospitable. (Despite my occasional—and usually futile—efforts to convince myself otherwise, what people think of me is something I can't not care about.) But also because such questions have the potential to lead a conversation to new depths.

The question of where a person is from is fascinating on many levels. Ask it, and chances are, you've been there.

So at the very least, you can talk about that while you're pouring.

Vancouver? Really? I'm from there too. What part of the city do you live in? I'm in Mount Pleasant.

And did you want to start with the Pinot Gris?

In a tasting room, that may be as far as the conversation goes in terms of place. But if you sit across a table from a friend to enjoy wine over a meal, the possibility of mutual knowing increases dramatically.

Curiosity plus time equals more curiosity.

"Where did you grow up?"

I recently shared a meal with a new pal, and we got to talking about places we'd lived. At one point he asked, "Did you grow up here?" This is similar to "Where are you from?" and yet much different. When someone asks me where I grew up, I usually say, "Sort of all over the place." In the grand scheme of things, this is not totally accurate.

What I *mean* by "all over the place" is that I moved around more than the average person I've met. I went to nine different schools between kindergarten and grade twelve. Three of those were in grade one alone. During that time, I lived in eight different homes. And while the places in which I grew up were relatively close together—especially when you consider how big the world is—their climates were vastly different, both meteorologically and metaphorically. As these moves were happening, I didn't reflect on how they impacted me. But just as fine wine reveals new layers of complexity and depth over time, aging has opened my sense of wonder about how these places have formed who I am.

I was born in Vancouver, British Columbia. I lived with my family in nearby Burnaby until I was almost three.

Then we moved to Fresno, California, where I spent a number of my childhood years. Fresno is smack dab in the middle of the state. It's also in the middle of a desert. You can grow wine there, but barely. Head any further south inland, and it's simply too hot. Warm, sunny, and dry is pretty much the story year-round. Winter wasn't much of a thing at all. I don't ever remember seeing snow. And instead of maple and fir, the boulevards of Fresno were lined with palm trees. Since it was hot all the time, our neighbours all had pools in their backyards. As kids, we ran willy-nilly around the cul-de-sac without shoes on and without a second thought.

I have this vivid memory, from when I was around eight, of heading over to one of my friends' places on a hot, sunny afternoon for a dip in their pool. I arrived at his place. I reached out to ring the doorbell. And a black widow spider sat right next to it, less than an inch away. I tell myself it was definitely the poisonous kind.

That if I had touched it, I probably would have died.

Was that the moment I became afraid of spiders? I can't say for certain. Two things I do know:

1. That memory transports me to California.
2. That place acutely shaped my sense of fear.

After grade four, our family moved back to Canada—to Abbotsford, BC—where we stayed until I completed grade 10.

I also lived in Saskatoon, Saskatchewan, for a time, which is the opposite of a desert.[1] The stories I'd heard about the Canadian prairies were the ones you probably heard, too: a land cursed by perpetual winter, like Narnia under the spell of the White Witch. It's not true. They have summers, often glorious ones. But the winters are very long and cold. People literally plug in their cars so the engines don't freeze.

We moved there as I was heading into grade eleven. To my parents' credit, they prepared my brother and me well for it. Our first exposure to Saskatoon took place in the summer, and I have no doubt that this was an intentional move on the part of my folks. (Well played, Mom and Dad. *Well. Played.*)

Their timing was, perhaps, more important than they even knew because first impressions matter. Had I walked off the airplane and been met by a temperature of twenty below zero (minus forty with the windchill), I may have put up more of a fight against moving there.

First impressions matter, because this move was a tough one.

I wasn't always part of the most popular crowd, which was fine. But friends are a big deal when you're sixteen. It feels good to belong. In the summer of '87, I was finishing grade ten. After a couple of awkward years, with a face full of acne and a few bumpy romantic beginnings—

"Hey Jill, would you like to go to the Christmas banquet with me?"
"Well, I heard Damien might ask me, but if he doesn't, then sure."

—I'd found my people. I was in choir, jazz band, and basketball, and had good friends in each of those circles.

It was far from perfect. It was high school.

But to be uprooted from that place of security and belonging at my tender age was painful.

In what ways, and to what degree, did that particular change in geography contribute to my need to feel connected? I can't know for sure. But as I survey the relational ground I've walked throughout my life, these transitions are markers and signposts worth paying attention to.

Did the vastly different climates impact my upbringing? Did my geography shape who I've become? Obviously yes. So did yours. And so did many other factors:

> The books I read.
> The music I listened to, sang, and played.
> The artwork I experienced.
> The friendships I shared.
> The faith I inherited.

The question that remains is how. You don't have to be exhaustive about this. What matters is to acknowledge that the depth and richness of who we are as human persons is enhanced, appreciated, and brought into the open when we consider the many influences that shaped and formed us.

So, what does all this have to do with wine?

In his book, *A Vineyard in My Glass,* wine-merchant-turned-wine-writer Gerald Asher aims to show that "the meaning and pleasure of a wine lie always in the context of its origin and in the concurrence of where, how, and with whom we enjoy it."[2]

As one who spent a good portion of his life in the company of winegrowers, Asher writes:

> If I find in a wine no hint of where it was grown, no mark of the summer when the fruit ripened, and no indication of the usages common among those who made it, I am frustrated and disappointed. Because that is what a good, honest wine should offer. It is not just a commodity subjected to techniques to boost this or that element to meet the current concept of a marketable product.[3]

This broad description of origin, this total environment in which a wine is produced, is what the French refer to as *terroir* (tear–WAHR). A precise definition of terroir is tough to pin down. The way it's characterized can vary broadly. Often, discussions veer toward specific *elements* of terroir, such as soil, climate, sun exposure, altitude, slope, aspect, and a vineyard's proximity to water. Some believe that farming techniques, and even the histories of the winegrowers themselves, ought to be included in thoughts about terroir.

Philippe Courrian, owner of Château La Tour Haut-Caussan in Bordeaux said, "A wine should express the geology of the vineyard and the personality of the grower, not a formula of winemaking procedures and a list of barrel-makers' telephone numbers."[4]

However you define it, just about every winemaker thinks of terroir as the most crucial aspect of winemaking.[5] There also seems to be broad consensus that when we speak of terroir, we're talking about wine that evokes a sense of place.

American wine writer Matt Kramer calls it *somewhereness*.[6]

In his article "What Makes Wine a Landmark," Kramer asks:

> Isn't taste what fine wine is all about? Nope. You'd think it would be, but it's not so. Let me push this further: the purpose of fine wine is not to give pleasure, but to give insight... the greatest wines literally mark the land for us. They tell us something about the earth that we could not otherwise know. This is their pleasure, an insight so intrinsic that it endures and repeats itself over generations. Everything else is just, well, taste.[7]

Is Kramer right in saying that the insight we glean from wine is its primary pleasure? It's a bold claim, and you may not agree. But, the idea that a wine reveals much about its origins is worthy of reflection. As is the notion that this is wine's most pleasurable offering.

I'm part of a wine club that meets about once a month.[8] We sip wine. We eat cheese that's a bit fancier than mozzarella from Safeway. We visit, we laugh, we enjoy each other's company. And of course, we taste wine. But there's also an educational component. We learn about flavour profiles and winemaking techniques. We learn about the people who grow the wine and what drives them. We learn about the regions around the globe where these incredible wines are made. Without this learning, the pleasure of drinking the wine would be greatly diminished.

We crave insight.

Learning never takes away from appreciation. It enhances it. If you learn a few basic tips on how to approach the world of wine, you will treasure it more, not less. Learning about wine inevitably leads to a deeper exploration of place. Of somewhereness. The more you taste, the more you wonder. The more you discover, the more you ask, "Oh wow. Where is *this* from? How has that particular terroir produced what I'm tasting?"

And in my case, I started turning the question inward. Where am I from? How has place shaped who I am?

You and I are unmistakably linked to the 'soil' we grew up in.

The Maori, the Indigenous people of New Zealand, have a beautiful word for terroir—one that lies at the heart of their identity. *Tūrangawaewae* (pronounced toor-angha-why-why) means "a place to put your feet" or "a place to stand." Everyone has their own Tūrangawaewae. A place you're deeply connected to that informs and fuels your sense of personhood.[9]

Isn't that just stunning?

(I mean, I'm one who thinks that if you watch Disney's *Moana* and don't cry, you basically have no soul. The ocean *called* her, you guys.)

When I first read about Tūrangawaewae, I asked myself, "Is there a place to which I feel deeply connected?" Given that I grew up in various soils and not a single vineyard, I realize that there's a disconnect in me around the notion of somewhereness. Instead of an unbreakable bond with a particular place, my moving around resulted in a profound sense of all-over-the-place-ness.

How has this shaped me? Well, for one thing, I'm pretty flexible when life throws curveballs. As long as I'm healthy, I'm usually up for anything. But also, my all-over-the-place-ness has made me the sort of person who keeps asking how my past shaped who I've become. I recognize that there is no final, definitive answer to that question. It's something I get to continue discovering.

All-over-the-place-ness isn't a bad thing. Not at all. But the absence of a distinct somewhereness does make me long for a deeper sense of connection to a single place. It makes me wonder if I have my own Tūrangawaewae. If I do, where might it be?

I'm starting to feel like my Tūrangawaewae is the ocean (which may explain the whole Moana thing). The Pacific, in particular.

Yes, I realize the ocean is huge: more all-over-the-place than somewhere. But bear with me. Here's how I would name my connection to the ocean, which, on some level, has always been there:

I'm drawn to its spaciousness. I think a lot of people experience me as a spacious human. That when they're with me, there's room for them to be who they are.
I'm drawn to its mystery. How ocean depths contain an ecosystem filled with life we rarely, if ever, get to see. I try to show up in my relationships as someone who holds curiosity about what's beneath the surface of peoples' lives.

I'm drawn to its wildness and its unpredictability.
I'm drawn to its beauty, to the flow of the tides.

And I'm drawn to the way the ocean links us as humans. It reminds me that we're connected. That each and every earthling is dependent on water for our survival.

So, Nelson. Where are you from?

A bunch of places. I moved around a fair bit. But apart from a few years on the Saskatchewan prairies, I have never lived more than 100 miles from the Pacific Ocean.

The ocean is the closest thing I have to a Tūrangawaewae. The ocean is the through-line that helps me feel a sense of somewhereness amid my all-over-the-placeness.

Just as many components contribute to the somewhereness of a particular wine, a unique blend of countless variables make us who we are.

There are things we are aware of, like a fear of spiders or of girls named Jill, and others we may never know, hidden below the surface.

We grow up in families we didn't ask to be born into. They were given to us, and they became 'ours.' My experience of being in my family is uniquely mine. It's different from my brother's, my mom's, my wife's.

Besides all this, foundational understandings about human origins have been handed down to us. My own faith narrative tells me I was made in the image of a benevolent Creator. That there is something, Someone, beyond me who loves me. Who is always present and active in my life, infusing all my somewhereness with divine meaning.

As we take this journey together, we will discover that the subject of this book is neither wine nor spirituality.

It's you.
Me.
Us.

So, we've come to the end of chapter one. We've spent some time considering how place shapes who we are, just as a good wine speaks of the land that bore it.

We're about to move 'up' now, just slightly. To ascend from the soil, up the rootstock and into the vineyard itself. To break ground and breathe open air. But before we start down that path, you may want to pause and consider a few questions:

Think about the place you're from or the places where you grew up. Do you have a keen sense of somewhereness, or is there a bit of a disconnect for you too?

Do you have a Tūrangawaewae? Are you connected to one place in particular? If so, how is it expressed in who you are? How does that fruit get pressed through your memory and awareness?

Grab a journal, reflect, and make some tasting notes that might help you attend to your somewhereness.

When you're ready, turn the page and join me for a walk among the vines.

VINEYARD

CHAPTER TWO

The Fine Line

Grateful people learn to celebrate even amid life's hard and harrowing memories because they know that pruning is no mere punishment, but preparation.

—Henri Nouwen, *Turn My Mourning into Dancing*

It hurts for a bud to bloom.

—Martin Laird, *A Sunlit Absence*

"Where should I go this time? Have you tried anything new lately?"

These are questions I always ask my friend Pam, who lives in Oliver, BC. We managed to get up to the Okanagan during the Covid-19 pandemic, when travel restrictions didn't prevent us from doing so.

"You've gotta try *vinAmité*," she replied. Pam was always ready with a few good recommendations. "They're making some really lovely wines and have been getting some well-deserved attention lately."

I hadn't been there before, but was curious to sample their portfolio. So, I made an appointment. On this particular trip, I couldn't hit as many tasting rooms as I would have liked. This was largely due to Covid, which increased the necessity of booking appointments in advance. I felt compelled to make the most of this visit—to take my time, to learn what I could about that particular winery, and to prepare my palate.

I know what you're thinking, *Prepare your palate? You say you're not a wine snob, but come on.*

I get it. Palate prep might seem like next-level wine nerdery, but I assure you it's not. Let me explain.

During that same trip, I read *What Makes a Wine Worth Drinking* by Terry Theise (rhymes with "peace"). Besides being my favourite wine writer, Theise is also an American importer of boutique wines from Germany, Austria, and Champagne. Translation: he's a professional taster. As far as Theise is concerned, to do his work with integrity requires an unusual-for-the-rest-of-us degree of attention to what's going on with his palate. Especially when he's trying to determine which wines he may want to import for the North American market.

Theise writes, "I am notorious for not eating lunch on tasting days, much to the chagrin of anyone travelling with me, who eventually learns to pack sandwiches from the breakfast spread. I'm also ridiculously careful at breakfast; one itty-bitty slice of smoked salmon will falsify my palate for several hours. I'm militantly against chives for similar reasons."[1]

I can still hear your thoughts. *Sure, that makes sense for someone tasting and selecting wines for an entire continent. But there's no need for me to be that obsessive.*

Perhaps not. But Theise changed my mind (and I hope he'll change yours) when he offered this perspective: "Growers work a whole year to show me wines I'll taste for one or two minutes. The least I can do is take care that my palate isn't screwed up."[2]

I'm not Terry Theise.

On my highly anticipated tasting day (which consisted of exactly one winery, where I tried maybe four or five wines), not screwing up my palate meant not brushing my teeth again right before leaving the house. Also I did manage to avoid chives. The last thing I wanted was to sip a lovely Bordeaux-style blend that's supposed to taste like blackberry, plum, and vanilla, and all I'm getting is fresh mint Sensodyne.

The next time you pour yourself a glass of wine, look at it. Swirl it. Get your nose in the glass and give it a good sniff. (I humbly suggest that this is the least we can do as non-professional tasters. Even if we just brushed our teeth.) As you take your first sip, consider this: before fruit is harvested—before a single grape gets the life squeezed out of it—years of mindful, meticulous planning go into the sumptuous juice you hold in your hand:

assessing soil and climate
choosing the right grapes for the terroir
orienting rows
spacing and trellising vines
planting
watering
pruning
shoot thinning
protecting
canopy managing (aka *leafing,* that is, controlling the amount of sunlight and air the fruit clusters receive)
inspecting
crop thinning (this helps the vines direct their energy toward the best-quality clusters)
measuring sugar levels
watching
waiting
praying

All this happens in the vineyard.

Part of my apprenticeship included visits to several vineyards that produce fruit for Nk'Mip Cellars and other Arterra brands. My tour guide was Nelson Dutra, a vineyard manager responsible for 460 acres of vineyards in the south Okanagan.[3] Vineyard Boss Nelson had an engineering background but eventually shifted to viticulture and started working for Arterra in the early 2000s.[4] He had a solid reputation as a hard worker. One of his colleagues told me he would bust his butt 24/7 to get ready for harvest.

Vineyard Boss Nelson picked me up at Nk'Mip around nine in the morning. It was already warm outside and about to get warmer. He wore a faded black t-shirt, khaki jeans, and rugged-yet-comfortable work boots. We hopped in his truck and drove to Sunrock vineyard. Sunrock is a 180-acre vineyard on the Osoyoos Lake Bench. As we drove onto the site, I gasped at the monumental, south-facing granite outcropping that gives the vineyard its name. With a slope that also faces south, the pristine lake at the bottom, and its sheer size, seeing Sunrock for the first time meant I needed a minute to collect myself. It was astonishing. Vineyards like this are why many think of the Okanagan as Canada's Napa Valley.

Every choice made in winegrowing, or viticulture, affects what ends up in the bottle—including what to grow where, trellising, training, irrigation, and pest management.

"We're not in the business of growing grapes," Nk'Mip Senior Winemaker Randy Picton told me one day as we were walking in a different vineyard. "We're in the business of growing wine."[5] The decision of what to grow where—matching grapes to ground—is primary. When Sunrock was first planted in 1998 and 1999, the red varietals (types of grape) included 30 acres of Pinot Noir. Within a few years, it became clear that Sunrock was far too hot for Pinot. So those vines were grafted over to mainly Shiraz.[6]

Once they've got the right varietal, vineyard managers focus on curating the amount of crop they're going to harvest.

Three crucial steps in this curation are *pruning, shoot thinning,* and *crop thinning.*

PRUNING

If you leave a grapevine to its own devices, it will eventually show you the meaning of the word sprawl. It will travel the world, spread itself far and wide, and produce as many leaves and as much fruit as it possibly can. You might think, *More grapes? Awesome! Isn't that what you want?* Not exactly, no. When vines are left unchecked, they yield more fruit than winegrowers want. If the crop is too big, it can ripen unevenly, giving you fruit that lacks the intensity of flavour needed to make great wine. This is why you need to prune. Pruning directs the vine's energy so you end up with a smaller amount of the best fruit possible. It occurs between growing seasons, sometime in late winter or early spring, when vines are still dormant. The actual work of pruning involves removing canes (woody branches at least two years old) and spurs (younger branches, usually one year old). *How* pruning happens depends largely on the framework used to support a vine's growth, such as a trellis, an arbour, or a pergola.

SHOOT THINNING

A second crucial aspect of vineyard care is known as shoot thinning. It happens early in the growing season. A shoot is the primary unit of vine growth. It contains stems, leaves, tendrils, and fruit. Shoots are where the action is, which is why they get heaps of attention from vineyard managers.

When Vineyard Boss Nelson and I got to Sunrock, the workers were shoot thinning. Nelson explained the process: "Once the pruning framework is set up, once the shoots start popping, we want to get our shoot count down to our desired target. To make sure we're not getting huge, contested areas where we have a whole bunch of shoots and a bunch of congestion, so you get the sunlight and air penetration you want."

In essence, shoot thinning is about getting over-congested areas thinned down. It finishes the task that pruning began.

CROP THINNING

A little later during the growing season, another step is required. Crop thinning, also known as cluster thinning or cluster removal, refers to removing flower and grape clusters on the vine. One reason to thin clusters is that vines have too much crop and there isn't enough leaf area to ripen the crop as desired. This is often caused by poor shoot growth. If this happens, removing the fruit early enough gives the vine more time to ripen the crop that remains. Another reason for crop thinning is when you have good balance between crop and leaf, but the winemaker believes the wine could be better if you had less crop per vine.

As we continued our walk through Sunrock, Vineyard Boss Nelson talked about other management techniques and practices. "Irrigation is pretty important," he said. This sounded like an understatement. "Winemakers typically want smaller berries with a high skin-to-juice ratio. They frown on pumped up, bloated berries." The reason for this is that many of the flavour profiles and colours present within wine are produced by the skins. For example, with red varieties, skins need to sit with the pulp for a week to get the colour extraction and a lot of the flavours.

Vineyard Boss Nelson explained that the main goal during this early phase of the growing season is to try and keep your plants happy until fruit set. That is, when the flowers begin to form berries. Once that happens, he said, "We throttle back the water and tread the fine line between starving the plants to death and giving them enough to encourage continued ripening." A vineyard can't just coast its way to fruitfulness. Vines have their own work to do as well, like sending their roots deeper into the soil where they can find nourishment.

Each of these choices impacts the quality, character, and style of what ends up in your glass. Are you beginning to see why prepping your palate for a tasting may not be such a crazy idea?

What struck me most from my time among the vines is that there are countless decisions to be made to grow them well. And each of these decisions falls along a spectrum between careful attention and tough love.

It's a fine line. A tricky balance.
As a lot of important work tends to be.

We could also say it this way: good vineyard management is both the vinegrower *doing things* to the vines and allowing the vines to *do their own work.*

The latter makes me think of taking final exams in high school. The kind you have to write in the gym, away from the comfort of your regular classroom. You sit in a long row of desks, nervous and jittery, maybe even a bit guilty, because you should have studied more. The teacher plops a big stack of papers on the desk of the first person in each row, to hand backwards. And then she pushes her glasses up on her nose and says in a nasal voice, "You've got 90 minutes to complete the test. Hand it in up here when you're done. Eyes on your own paper. Good luck."

Eyes on your own paper.
This is your work. No hitchhiking on someone else's.
When you cheat, you only cheat yourself.

Your work. *Yours.*

In the vineyard that is your life, what does it look like to do your own work?

A lot of the work I have tried to attend to over the past decade or so has been *inner work.* It's been about honesty. About speaking up when I have an opinion rather than remaining passive. Learning that I have a voice.

I'm a Nine on the Enneagram. The Enneagram is an ancient personality typing system. It identifies nine types (*ennea* means nine) that are expressed individually and in relation to others. Since I was introduced to it over a decade ago, I have come to appreciate it a great deal. Not only as a tool for understanding my own behaviours and motivations, but for learning how such self-awareness can help make my relationships healthier.

Being a Nine, I tend to merge with other people's agendas, feelings, and viewpoints to keep the peace in both my inner and outer worlds. I am prone to forget that my unique perspective not only counts but matters. It matters that others hear it, and it matters that I share it.

Like when a group of people try to make a group decision about where to go for lunch and ask my preference. Sometimes I don't have an opinion on the matter. Truly. At least, not a particularly strong one. I might say something like, "I'm easy. I could go either way."

Other times I may well have an opinion. A good one. A strong one. One where I know that if I don't say something, I'll need to be prepared to live with some disappointment or lingering frustration.

Also, I've learned that Nines have the least amount of energy of any number on the Enneagram, so maybe I'm just too tired to make a decision. If it's this last one, rather than risk the conflict that may arise from people disagreeing with me or thinking my opinion is stupid, I'd opt for an, "I dunno. Where do you guys wanna go?"

Do you know what I'm talking about?
Any other Nines out there feel me?

I used to get a daily email called *Enneathought for the Day.*
One morning when I was writing this chapter, my customized Type Nine Enneathought was: "Growth does not come from

being just an easygoing, likeable person. Growth comes from allowing your ego's story to drop away."

On point.

The ego, or what some spiritual writers call the *false self,* would love nothing more than to keep living as though my whole identity centred on being perceived as a calm, unflappable person everyone likes. When I silence that narrative, I begin to discover the deeper truth of who I am. I begin to tap into my true self.

Whether you're a Nine or not (or even know/care about the Enneagram), if you can relate at all, you know how great it feels when you find the courage to share what you truly think. Even if it's only about where to eat.

I remember a time when a group of out-of-province friends were in town for a conference. The evening session ended and a few of them started to think about where we might go grab a pint and a bite.

They invited me to come along. I asked where we were going. Steamworks, they said. In Gastown, they said.

If you know Vancouver, you know that Gastown is an historic neighbourhood. It's where the city as we know it began. Cobblestone streets, wrought-iron lamp posts, and some great places to grab a bite or a pint. Also tons of tourists. I understood the appeal, particularly for out-of-towners, but I confess there's a special place in my heart for Gastown. I also got why Steamworks was the intended choice. It's close to the Skytrain. They've got a great menu, some fine craft beer, and stunning views of the Burrard Inlet.

(You didn't think I was only into wine, did you?)

But this was my town. And I knew that while they weren't making a *bad* choice, they also weren't making the best choice. Know what I mean? I could have been quite content to spend the evening at Steamworks. But it's also possible we could have ended up next to a table filled with some loud-mouthed Australian rugby team who happened to be in town. It would have been fine. Truly. I'm not just saying that as a Compliant Nine. But something inside was telling me that if I didn't speak up, my contentment would have been at least 37% inauthentic.

Something else was going on as well. These were my guests. I felt responsible to host them well. I only had this one chance since they were all heading home the next day. Not to get too dramatic, but whenever I think back on this moment, a song from the musical Hamilton courses through my soul: *I am not giving away my shot.*

"Guys," I said, "I'd love to join you. But let's go to *The Alibi Room* instead. It's like, 10 minutes further away. We'll get to see more of Gastown since we'll walk through it. The tap selection is incredible. And on top of that, you'll get to taste the best dang burger in the city."

That got their attention. They were more than willing to change course and defer to my opinion. *Mine.* I felt valued, appreciated, like I mattered. We went to The Alibi Room. Best burgers were had. Great beer was imbibed. Stories were swapped and laughter was shared. It was a memorable night spent among friends.

In large part, this happened because, at that moment, I refused to go with the flow, to hitchhike on someone else's opinion to avoid conflict. I did my own work.

Now some reading this might think, *You call that work? Beer and burgers?*

Yup. It is work. *My work.*

Which means it's not necessarily the same as yours.

Here's another example—one where the stakes were considerably higher than choosing a lesser pub.

It's 2009. I'm neck-deep in preparing to launch a new faith community in Vancouver with the help of a generous network that facilitates the start of new churches. Like most non-profits, this network was supported significantly by donations from people who believe in the work.

Without that network and its supporters, our new church wouldn't have even made it to fruit set.

Our church had only been around for a few months, when I got cc'd on a group email sent to all church planters. The email asked for statistics on how many people attended our gatherings, how many people had come to faith, and how many people we'd baptized. They called it a Sunday Dashboard. And we were to submit these numbers every month so they could be shared with constituents who supported our work. So they could "celebrate the work God was doing through us."

You might read that and think: *Totally fair. They are paying your salary, after all.* I read it and thought, *This is ludicrous. What have I done? This is not what I signed up for.*

I felt like I was on the show *Arrested Development: I've made a huge mistake.*

Why did I feel that way? Because regardless of what was *intended,* what I *heard* was that I was to submit monthly statistics to prove the legitimacy of my work. Work that was messy, slow, and ridiculously hard to quantify. I was afraid they would think I wasn't measuring up. I felt anxious to report low numbers. Or worse, to report zeroes. Frustrated and disappointed, I doubted my calling and regretted everything.

I had inner work to do.
So, I did something I'd heard of people doing, but I'd never done before.

But first, I spent 24 hours cooling down.

Then, I wrote a stream-of-consciousness, unedited, completely honest letter to my direct supervisor. I mean, all the feelings.

Apparently, some people never send the letter. Instead, the writing acts as a means of sorting out their emotions. Get the feelings out through pen and paper. Be as raw as you need to be. But don't deliver the note. I saw the wisdom in this practice. So I wrote with the intention to feel my feelings. It was a hard process, but it felt good. I named some things that needed naming. I was respectful of my leaders and the network, but also respected myself enough to be honest about how the Sunday Dashboard was landing with me.

I booked a meeting with my supervisor for the following week, still unsure whether I would use the letter in any way.

When we sat down at Starbucks, I thought, *Yeah, that whole writing-but-not-sending thing? Nice "exercise," but not for me. I'm gonna send it.*

I read the letter out loud.

It wasn't easy, but it was one of the best decisions I'd ever made. Feelings were hurt. Offence was taken. We worked through it. The fruit on the other side of this conflict? A stronger bond.

43

Deeper understanding. Greater respect. And a better working relationship.

This was my work. Nobody could do it for me.

You have your own work.

It's up to you to figure out what it is. And then to decide each day, countless times, whether to engage with it or not.

Depending where you're at, the awareness of the need to find and attend to our own work can sound ominous and threatening. That's when it's good to realize that help is available.

We never do our own work in complete isolation.
A good vinegrower is never far away from her vines.

There's a beautiful and insightful documentary called *A Year in Burgundy*. In my view, it's well worth a watch whether you're into wine or not. At one point in the film, wine producer Lalou Bize-Leroy, known as the Queen of Burgundy, speaks candidly about her relationship to her vineyard:

> Of course, I know my vines! When they don't see me, they're unhappy. When I arrive, they're happy. I really love my vines. Vines are not well understood. You have to put yourself in their place. You have to understand why they're not doing well. You have to be part of the life of the vine, and the life of the soil too. That's all you've got to do. Of course, I believe in biodynamics. We should cut out all chemical substances. The herbicides, the insecticides, the fungicides, the pesticides, all the -icides. They sound just like homicide! We should stop killing things and give them the life force instead.

There is an intimacy between humans and vines. One that requires a deep knowledge of what is most needed at any given time. There are times, for example, when giving them the life force looks and feels a lot more like tough love.

The Queen of Burgundy's former winemaker, Dd Poncheret, put it this way (also in the film and in French):

> A vine has to suffer...to make good grapes. You can't coddle it, or it will become lazy like a couch potato. He sits there and you feed him. He doesn't have to work. If the roots don't dig deep, there's trouble. They have to go down four or five metres. Then if it's dry for a couple of months, no problem. The vine will survive. A vine can live 100 years if you treat it right.

I really love my vines,
and
A vine has to suffer.

It's a fine line.

This work isn't easy. It's hard to love well, and it's hard to suffer.
Good wine doesn't just happen. It's hard work.
And it's hard work to grow.

If you've spent any time in or near the Christian church, you know that wine is kind of a big deal in Scripture. When Jesus was about to suffer and die out of love for humanity, he invited his closest followers to share a meal. He took bread to symbolize his body. He broke it and gave it to his disciples. Wine represented his lifeblood, freely poured out. Many people are familiar with this.

What is less well-known is that Jesus also had a fair amount to say about vines and branches. In fact, vineyard imagery in Scripture even predates Jesus. It goes way back to ancient Israel and the Hebrew scriptures. There, we come to see that a healthy vineyard symbolizes flourishing.

There's this moment in one of the gospels when Jesus is nearing the time of his suffering. He says to his followers, *"I am the true vine, and my Father is the gardener. He cuts off every branch in me that bears no fruit, while every branch that does bear fruit he prunes so that it will be even more fruitful."* [7]

This is a picture of Divine shoot thinning.

Have you ever pictured God as a gardener? I sure have. It's one of my favourite images. Even more so since writing this book. I imagine God walking up and down the rows, saying *Yes, I know my vines. When they don't see me, they're unhappy. When I arrive they're happy. I really love my vines.*

What if God is like a gardener, pruning and thinning out the over-congested areas of our lives, out of a desire for fruitfulness? According to Jesus, that is exactly what God is like. That changes things a bit, doesn't it?

Staying with the vineyard image, remember how the vineyard manager prunes, thins, and waters the vines? Remember how the vines need to work hard to send their roots deep into the soil? These verses say something about the Divine Parent's role as vineyard manager. And in this picture, Jesus is the vine. What's our role as branches?

"Remain in me, as I also remain in you," Jesus says. *"No branch can bear fruit by itself; it must remain in the vine. Neither can you bear fruit unless you remain in me."* [8]

What's our work?

Remain.
Stay put.
Don't leave.

The Greek word there is *meno*. Abide, stay connected.

Ready for one more verse? *"I am the vine; you are the branches. If you remain in me and I in you, you will be given the life force..."* (That last bit is my new preferred paraphrase.)

And here's the kicker: *"...apart from me you can do nothing."*[9]

Keep in mind that this is happening near the end of Jesus' earthly life. It's common for people nearing death to reflect on and say the things that matter most. They want their final words to count. I believe it's no different here.

If we take Jesus' words at face value, that "nothing" even *includes our own work.* We can't prune ourselves. The strength, impetus, desire, and discipline to engage our pruning come from outside ourselves. The "life force" sometimes takes the form of grace to be received. Our task is to stay close to the Source.

There are things the vineyard manager does, and there is work that is ours to do. All of it is for fruitfulness and flourishing. Not to mention transformation. We're not growing grapes, we're growing wine. Growth means change.

And because change is the goal, and change can be hard, sometimes the work (even with the help of the Divine Gardener) is painful. A vine has to suffer.

So. Time for some reflection. Here are some questions that may be helpful:

What is your work? Let me encourage you not to dodge the stuff that seems hardest—the work you've been avoiding because it's painful, because you'll have to suffer through it. It may be that this isn't the right time to engage your work like you know you need to, but you could make a plan. Remember that whatever you have to do, life and new possibilities are on the other side. As Alanis Morrisette put it in a deep cut that almost no one has ever heard but is still awesome: "The only way out is through. The faster we're in, the better."

Where is there over-congestion in your life? Is your energy being directed and focused where it ought to be? What needs to be pruned, trimmed, or cut back? Is there too much noise, be it inner distortion or clamour from outside? In the age of podcasts and TED Talks (both of which I love), is there a chance you may be overcropped from listening to too many voices? Ask yourself: Do I need another motivational expert right now?

Our primary work needs to be tending to the truth contained within, which has been planted there by our Divine Gardener. Sometimes our work is to turn down the volume so we can actually listen. To make friends with silence. Silence is the universally-required precursor to doing deep soul work.

Or maybe our work is more like eliminating clutter, doing less, taking a break, moving slower. Removing distractions so you can tend to what's really there—you know, like not coating your entire oral cavity with Sensodyne when you're about to sip Bordeaux.

Right after I got the Sunday Dashboard email from my church planting supervisor, I looked up at my bookshelf and saw two books sitting side-by-side that couldn't be more at odds: *Planting*

Fast-Growing Churches and *The Art of Pastoring*. There are times when speed and efficiency may well be required of us. Other times, what is truly needed is something more pastoral—in the countryside, rural, agrarian sense.[10]

What might it look like to remain close to the Source of Life in this season? What practices will help you remember it's not all up to you? That even getting down to your work depends on Grace? What habits and rhythms remind you who you are: that you are good, that you are beloved, that you are enough? What habits and rhythms serve to remind you who Jesus is: the True Vine, apart from whom we can do nothing? Perhaps letting your roots go deep could look like adding some ancient, "classic" disciplines: reading and meditating on Scripture; praying the Psalms, the Lord's Prayer, or the Daily Office; taking up communion, fasting, silence.

Maybe you need to expand your definition of what counts as spiritual practice. What practices open you to receive the nutrients of the Spirit of God? Maybe it's listening to or playing music, or hiking, or running, or kayaking, or drawing.

Maybe it's wine tasting. (What!?)

Dd Poncheret, the winemaker I quoted earlier, also gave this advice to vineyard managers: "Even if there's no work to do...you must go and visit your vines. That's the important thing. There's always something you'll discover."

Presence always matters. It's crucial in caring for growing things.
Or people.
Or your own soul.

How might the Gardener want to visit you today?

CHAPTER THREE

Little Foxes

Catch us the foxes,

the little foxes,

that ruin the vineyards—

for our vineyards are in blossom.

—**Song of Solomon 2:15**

It's a dangerous business, Frodo, going out your door.

You step onto the road, and if you don't keep your feet,

there's no knowing where you might be swept off to.

—**J.R.R. Tolkien**

As the rest of the wine world slowly discovers the beauty and potential of British Columbia's Okanagan Valley, industry professionals from more famous regions are taking note. An expert from Burgundy recently purchased a vineyard on the Naramata Bench.[1] A wealthy Chinese businessman is spending millions to set up a new high-volume operation on the Black Sage Bench.[2] Producers from the Old World are seeking new treasure in Canadian soil.

Severine Pinte is a French winemaker who came to BC in 2010, where she currently works as a winemaker, viticulturist, and managing partner at both *Le Vieux Pin* in Oliver and *La Stella* in Osoyoos.

I asked Pinte what her most significant culture shock was since coming to Canada.

"The dangerous wildlife," she said, "because our cultivated land is so small compared to the vast area around us. We have black widow spiders and rattlesnakes, more deer than we see in France, as well as bears that come down to threaten my grapes at harvest time. I didn't expect to see this."

Bears, y'all.

For King Solomon, foxes ruined the vineyards.
For Pinte, it's black bears with finely-tuned palates.

The next time you pour a bold, velvety glass of Merlot, imagine what wild beasts once ominously threatened what you now enjoy.

In the last chapter, we considered vineyard management techniques, like pruning and shoot thinning. Practices that, while they allow the vines to suffer, are done on purpose. They're meant to focus a vineyard's energy to curate the desired yield. But does growth only crop up when intentionality is a factor?

What about the setbacks and surprises the vinegrower doesn't intend but must watch out for and try to minimize? What about pests that range from the very large, like black bears and deer, to the very small, like fungal infections such as powdery mildew?

How do you sustain growth when little foxes are on the loose?

Let's hold these questions as we take another walk among the vines.

During my apprenticeship at Nk'Mip, my ten working days included two in the vineyards, one with a viticulturist and another with a vineyard manager.[3] Let me restate how far I am from an expert on vines and vineyards. Caveat aside, let me share a few things I learned.

One thing that struck me was the superhuman level of awareness vine growers must possess. Their role is to invest attention, knowledge, and expertise to plant and maintain healthy vineyards, so that grapes can be grown and harvested to produce marketable, good quality wine. A keyword in that sentence is *healthy*. Growers of grapes need to be constantly on the lookout for anything that might impede, stunt, threaten, or inhibit their vines from doing their best work.

The vineyard experts I spent time with seemed to have an encyclopedic knowledge of how vineyards work. Makes sense. But it was incredible to witness, even over two days.

We've already begun to discover how every decision made in the vineyard impacts the end product. Which is a daunting realization.

Caring for a vineyard is not unlike being a parent.
It's one thing to see a cute kid on a playground and think, "That's

easy. I could *totally* do that." It's quite another to skillfully embody the role of parenting.

You have to be dedicated and committed. You have to be in it for the long haul because this is slow work.

I will never fully understand why I still need to remind my daughter, Adriana, who is six, to use her fork or spoon at mealtime. She knows what we expect of her because we tell her, multiple times a day:

Use your fork.
Use your fork.
Use your fork.

Unless it's pizza or hot dogs for dinner, she sees my wife and me use utensils regularly and without fail. This girl just likes to use her hands. Occasionally, she will pick up her fork without our asking and let me tell you, it is a *moment*. "Adri! You used your fork! We're so proud!"

Cutlery: a constant reminder that the work of parenting is painstakingly slow.

It's slow work to continuously remind your kids to use their fork, flush the toilet, or put their stuffies away.

It's slow work to repeatedly say, "Oh, could you please try that again?" when they forget to say please or thank you, or they just have a *tone*.

It's slow work to stay committed to the bedtime routine night after night, even though it might seem easier to let them stay up, or skip the bath or the reading.

You need good, reliable circles of support. Since my wife and I became parents, my Mom and Dad have been incredible sounding boards, wise dispensers of advice, and shoulders to cry on. It makes sense that they're good at protecting, tending, and nurturing. They've been outfoxing foxes that threaten their children's well-being for half a century.

To parent well, you also need to cultivate humility. First, to build the muscles required to recognize when you need help. And then to ask for it. (The root of humility is *humus*, which is about dirt, earth, groundedness. Well. Interesting.)

You have to be willing to give up significant amounts of leisure time. (Can I get an amen, fellow parents?)

I remember the days when I used to head home from the office and was truly off for the rest of the night. I'd clock out at five and be *done*. Terri and I would prepare a meal together, super romantic. Maybe a new Jamie Oliver recipe we were anxious to try. Or, if we were feeling adventurous, a fancy curry from Vij's cookbook.[4] Either way, we didn't care if we ate at 5:30pm or 7:30pm. It didn't matter because, for more than 18 years, the entire evening was ours.

For the past six years, 5pm has signalled the start of the toughest shift of the day. The worst part is, you never know exactly when it'll be over. You could get lucky and be done by seven. Or you could sweat it out 'til nine.

When a parent talks about protecting *those precious evening hours,* this is what they're talking about.

Children require constant attention, devotion, and protection.

So do even the smallest vineyards.

A vinegrower is both gardener and doctor. Like a seasoned green thumb, they need to know what best contributes to life and vitality. At the same time, like an experienced medical professional, they need to possess an ongoing awareness of all that would keep a grapevine from flourishing. But it doesn't stop at knowing stuff. Action must follow awareness.

Vinegrowers need to be out among the vines, always on the lookout for possible problems. As Pinte put it, "I think it's important, going up and down the rows. My vineyard manager always checks for water stress, disease, and leafhoppers. There's a constant rhythm of observation—report—observation—report, and then if there's a threat, to determine the action needed."

And then take that action. The goal, of course, is continued growth and ongoing health.

Threats to a vineyard's growth aren't always easy to see, as with bears, birds, and deer. Often the most serious ones are smaller and more insidious. In the Okanagan Valley and most other wine regions around the globe, one of the most common threats to vineyard health is a nasty pest known as cutworm.

Cutworm is a term used to describe the larvae of many species in the moth family *Noctuidae* (pronounced "knock TO-a-day").[5] Biologically, they're not actually worms but caterpillars. As their family name suggests, these sneaky little insects are nocturnal. Most feed on weeds, but some climb the stems of plants to chomp on buds and other young foliage. In vineyard settings, you have to watch out for the climbers.

Here's how they wreak their havoc on grapevines.

Early in the growing season, as the weather starts to warm, these tiny climbing larvae feast on budding grapes, hollowing out their buds before the grapes can grow. Cutworms tend to concentrate on a smaller area. They'll eat a bud or two at night, head back down, and then back up the vine for more the next night.

"Bed and breakfast," Vineyard Boss Nelson called it. "You win some; you lose some. Everyone's gotta eat." A surprisingly compassionate response to these wily, annoying, murderous creatures.

Cutworms are a serious threat because young, greedily guzzled grapes often don't grow back at all. Or if they do, they grow back later than the rest of the crop, which can cause inconsistent ripening. And that, of course, impacts the overall quality of the wine.
To see the larvae in action, you need to shift into stealth mode and take a late-night walk among the vines. But this isn't totally necessary. The damage they cause is easily observable if you show up the morning after. Vineyard managers need their beauty sleep, too.

On the day I spent with Vineyard Boss Nelson, he got a call from one of his vineyard managers. From the concerned look on Nelson's face, I could tell this manager was in a bit of a panic. Apparently, the pesky *Noctuidae* had been unusually ravenous in one corner of a vineyard. The worker had counted 98 buds eaten within five or six panels (the space between posts). This would have been record damage, had it been accurate. Fortunately, 98 buds were the total amount eaten within an entire row, which is typically about 10 or 12 panels long. So, significant damage, but not as serious as it might have been. And still, something to keep an eye out for. You might dodge a bullet one night, but cutworms don't give up easily. They'll be back.

We're not all parents, but we all have children in our lives, to one degree or another. On top of that, we have all been children. And within each of us is an inner child. An inner child who is still healing from past wounds. An inner child who deserves our ongoing, compassionate attention and care.

Here's the question I'm inviting you to hold with me: What are some of the emotional, psychological, spiritual equivalents of cutworm? And how might they affect the development of a child?

My wife, Terri, is a trained Early Childhood Educator. She has extensive experience working in that field, including preschool classrooms, one-on-one tutoring, and daycare centres. She's really good at what she does.

When I asked Terri about cutworms and childhood, the first thing she thought of was the absence of touch.

Put positively, when we think of what most contributes to the healthy social-emotional-intellectual growth of children, the presence of touch is a huge factor.

"If you don't hug or show affection to a child," she said, "even if they have everything else, it can be problematic for their future. The lack of touch can severely inhibit their growth in the long term."

Research has shown that babies who are not held, nuzzled, and hugged enough can stop growing. And if adequate touch is with-held long enough, they can even die.[6]

As adoptive parents, our adoption agency drilled into Terri and me how critical it is to cultivate healthy attachment with your child. This is a basic need for every child, of course, but especially for children with adoptive parents. So in our case, it was important for Adriana—who didn't hear our voices while in the womb—to form a bond with us that included consistent, caring physical touch and affection.

When Terri was working in infant and toddler care, she and her colleagues had the opportunity to care for a boy I'll call Brayden. Brayden was a two-and-a-half-year-old who was left alone when he was too young to be left alone. As a result, he couldn't talk. He couldn't toilet train. He had limited ability to interact socially. With this awareness, his caregivers prioritized things like continual eye contact and maintaining a physical presence as the child napped. Anything to assure Brayden that he didn't have to worry while he was with them. That he could count on people who love him to be there.

If a child's basic need for touch isn't met, they simply cannot grow, learn, or flourish. Recognizing all this makes me more passionately committed to preemptive maintenance through touch. For my daughter's well-being, definitely. But also my wife's. And my own.

As Gandalf said to his young companion, "It's a dangerous business, Frodo, going out your front door."

It's a dangerous business being a grapevine.
And it's a dangerous business being human.

Little foxes—threats to our growth and flourishing, both conspicuous and cunning—are all around us. What can we do when things go wrong, when something is taken from us, when our early growth is impeded? What does preemptive maintenance look like? What can we learn from sound viticultural practice?

While apprenticing at Nk'Mip, I spent a day with Mike Watson, a viticulturist. Watson oversees more than fifty growers in the Okanagan Valley who provide grapes on contract for Arterra. Viticulturist Mike and I visited six farmers that day. I got to walk through vineyards while he checked on the state of buds and vines early in the growing season.

Of the six, my favourite was Andy the Hungarian. Andy was in his eighties. His wife had died a few years prior, and he was now living alone. Despite some minor health setbacks, Andy still preferred to maintain his two-acre vineyard himself, with no hired help.

Andy the Hungarian was fair-skinned and nearly bald. He wore a loose-fitting black t-shirt, baggy Dockers, and comfy sandals with black socks. Andy had weathered hands, a thick accent, and a hearty laugh. I thought, "This, right here, is what a good farmer looks like." I looked in awe as he stood proudly among his vines, where, as far as I know, he still grows Gewurztraminer and Chardonnay with a meticulous, loving hand. Even though he prunes and trims a bit slower than he once did. (It's all slow work anyway, remember.)

While Andy and Mike discussed matters beyond my expertise, I took a little stroll up and down the rows by myself. In one section, something caught my attention that I'd never seen in a vineyard before: bright yellow flowers on plants about a foot tall, growing vigorously between the vines.

I asked Viticulturist Mike what they were. "That's wild mustard," he said. And then explained that wild mustard is a beautiful, vibrant yellow weed that grows naturally between the vines.

It also happens to be a lethal weapon against cutworms.

When Andy the Hungarian started out as a farmer, he learned

he'd be forced to battle the Noctuidae. Andy was ready for it. Committed to it. Night after night he'd wake, long before sunrise, then walk to the vineyard and ultra-carefully pluck worms from branches by the light of his headlamp. Andy did this for a long time before he realized that the Noctuidae actually liked the taste of wild mustard more than young grape buds.

I can't pretend to know the actual taste comparison. But if those weeds are to grape buds as Doritos are to kale chips, who can blame the cutworms? As it happens (twist!), the weeds are toxic to many species of cutworm. They'll die if they eat too much. (Alas, the Doritos comparison holds up.)

Who knew that the antidote to a major vineyard threat would grow, naturally, right up beside the vines?

After I met Andy the Hungarian and learned about wild mustard, I thought of a story Jesus told, about a field where good and bad things grew at the same time.[7] Jesus seemed to be saying that the world is a jumble of different circumstances and events and that until we learn to see deeply, we won't know which is which.

At one point in the story, a student asks Jesus if he should pull out the weeds.

"No," Jesus answers. "Let them both grow together until the harvest."[8] At the end of the day, it's God's job to sort out what is wheat and what is a weed.

I love Richard Rohr's comment on this story:

> This is really quite risky of God—and it takes tremendous courage on our part to trust God and ourselves here. We are all a mixture of weeds and wheat and we always will be...We are simultaneously saint and sinner. That's the mystery of

holding weeds and wheat together in our one field of life. Acknowledging both the wheat and weeds in us keeps us from thinking too highly of ourselves and also from dismissing ourselves as terrible.[9]

It's all a dangerous business, being mixed-bag humans. Being a vineyard. But we keep doing it anyway. We keep planting vines. We keep growing ourselves. We keep becoming parents and caregivers.

Why, though?
If it's so dangerous, why do we do it?

Because it's all worth it, despite the danger.

So long as we tend to it, the vineyard produces grapes that will, in time, become wine fit for a feast. Our lives, too, hold the possibility of beauty, hope, forgiveness, and love.

To carry that potency forward toward its desired yield, we must do the inner work. (This is what we looked at in Chapter 2.)

At the same time, there is outer work we need to do—to catch the little foxes that would impede our growth. It's a dangerous business, so we keep protective measures in place.

We need salt-of-the-earth, leathery-handed farmer pals who are willing to don headlamps in the middle of the night to pluck caterpillars from our faces.

We need Saturday work teams to put on coveralls and tool belts, to help build fences that keep the deer out.

We need our mothers and fathers—adoptive, biological, spiritual—to teach us the slow work of parenting.

And we need Grace to allow ourselves to keep growing, as a mix of weeds and wheat, until the harvest.

HARVEST

CHAPTER FOUR

The Big Crush

Outside in the fields, the first signs of autumn are appearing. The vine-leaves have done their work for the year. They've harvested the sun, they've created the grapes. Now, they die. Every year, it's a spectacular show.

—David Kennard (writer), *A Year in Burgundy*

The fruitfulness of our lives shows itself in its fullness only after death. We ourselves seldom experience our fruitfulness. This is the mystery of Jesus' death and of the deaths who lived in his Spirit. Their lives yield fruit far beyond their short and often localized existence.

—Henri Nouwen, *Our Greatest Gift*

If you haven't skipped any pages, you'll know by now that my hands-on wine education began with a month-long apprenticeship at *Nk'Mip Cellars* in Osoyoos, Canada. That was in May, early in the growing season. A little over a year later, in October, I returned to *Nk'Mip* for a week to help with harvest.

My growing season exposure was rich and full, but I knew there was something special about being part of the harvest. It's basically a rite of passage for anyone who works in the industry.

Harvest is a critical moment. Before picking the fruit, winemakers want to wait for optimal ripeness for the style of wine they want to make. Deciding when it's go-time is probably the most crucial decision in the entire winemaking process. There would be less stress in making that call if every varietal[1] ripened at the exact same pace. But alas, they do not. For example, Cabernet Sauvignon needs more time to ripen than Chardonnay. Riesling tends to take longer than Pinot Noir.

Pace of ripening is one factor.
Weather is another.

Harvest would be a walk in the vineyard if you could predict and control the weather. Again, this is not an option available to anyone.

Join me in a little thought experiment, will you? Let's say you're a winemaker who is working with the four varietals I mentioned above, and you sit down to do some pre-harvest planning. Unless something totally unforeseen happens, you know you're going to harvest Pinot and Chardonnay first, Cab and Riesling later.

You map that out on your calendar.
You check the forecast and make any projected adjustments.
You line up your crews. (Whether you're hand-picking, machine-

harvesting, or both, humans are involved.)
You wait.
You go out and check the grapes repeatedly.
You keep asking yourself, "Are we there yet?"

It's getting close to go-time for your Pinot. You booked your crew.
You're ready. But upon closer inspection, you decide it could benefit from another five days on the vine.

You check the forecast again.

You learn that, unexpectedly, a heavy rainstorm is on the way.
Now you're faced with a decision: Do you leave your precious
grapes hanging when it's likely they'll be diluted and bloated by
the storm? Some might even burst open. Most winemakers will
not want to take that risk. Instead, they'll get out there at the last
possible moment before the rain hits, to pick the fruit and get it
to safety.

Safety means getting the grapes to the cellar to be pressed into juice.

The Big Crush.

That juice then travels to a larger vessel, such as a stainless steel
tank. Soon after, the fermentation process begins.

Most of my harvest experience was from the cellar side. I missed
the drama of timetabling and weather watching. But even so, I
knew I wanted to witness and extract whatever I could from this
part of the winegrowing process. Even if only for a week. It would
be hard, physical work. It would be the most literal opportunity
to get my hands dirty.

All these factors made harvest a must.

With the time approaching, I started to get excited and wanted to do everything I could to prepare. But our family was also moving house at the time, so I didn't have hour upon hour of discretionary time for geeking out on wine books or blogs. I had to multitask. One morning as I headed out on a run, I put the Bluetooth earbuds in and pulled up an especially nerdy (and therefore awesome) podcast called *Inside Winemaking,* hosted by Napa Valley winemaker, Jim Duane. I chose an episode that was specifically about harvest.[2]

In it, Jim was interviewing people who were changing careers and starting on a path to become winemakers. Among them was Ben Matthews, who, in response to a growing passion for winemaking, left a corporate day job to study and work a harvest with Jim. As Ben was telling the story of his first time crushing red grapes, he recalled Jim looking him in the eye and saying:

> Jim: This is an important day for you, Ben.
> Ben: Why is that, Jim? We got a lot of work to do or something?
> Jim: No. This is when the romance of winemaking can die.

How do you imagine the world of winemaking? What's your mental picture? A young woman in a flowing dress, glass in hand, walking down rows of vineyards? Perfectly backlit by the setting sun? Probably in Tuscany?

We've all seen the Instagram accounts of people who do an incredible job of showcasing the idyllic, harmonious, pleasurable side of the wine industry. And they should. As we'll discuss later, the end product is an exquisite treasure. A treasure to enjoy, to savour, to luxuriate in (within moderation—we'll talk about that soon as well).

But harvest is one moment in time where we can witness a high concentration of the toil, sweat, and tears that go into producing what we get to swirl, sniff and sip in tasting rooms and patios. Harvest is when the rose-coloured lens we see winemaking through starts to look less rosy. My experience certainly bore this out.

I spent nearly all my harvest time with Aaron Crey, who worked as the cellar supervisor at Nk'Mip for 17 years.[3] A cellar supervisor coordinates everything that happens in the cellar: crushing grapes, fermenting and fortifying juice, finishing, aging, and racking wine.[4] Aaron is part of the Cheam First Nation.

I really like Aaron. I always enjoyed working with him. Or at least I did, until day one of my Harvest Week, when he looked at me and said, "Alright, Nelson. Ready to do some punch-downs?"

I was excited. "Absolutely! Let's go for it!"

Foolish child.
I had no idea what I was in for.

Aaron led me to the red fermentation room, where three stainless steel tanks of Pinot Noir were inoculated the day before. This means yeast had been introduced, beginning the fermentation process: as the yeast goes to town on the sugars within the grape juice, they release alcohol and carbon dioxide as byproducts. Because Pinot Noir is a red grape, and the winemakers are producing red wine from it, what's in the tanks is not only *juice* but something called *must*.

Must comes from the Latin phrase *vinum mustum,* meaning "young wine," which, as you might expect, is precisely what it is: freshly pressed grape juice that contains the skins, seeds, and stems of the fruit. The solid portion of the must is formally known as *pomace* and typically makes up between 7-23% of the total weight of the must. Its less formal name is the *cap*. Call it a cap, if you must. (Wine puns need to be said out loud.)

As fermentation begins, winemakers engage various "cap manage-ment" techniques to extract colour, tannins, flavour, and aromas from the grape solids. One way to do this is via punch-downs.

According to expert Madeline Puckette, one of my favourite wine nerds and founder of *Wine Folly,* "Punch-downs...are a very del-icate way of stirring a wine."[5] Wine Folly is an essential online resource, maintained by the ever-witty Puckette. A sommelier friend told me about it when I took my initial wine appreciation deep dive and I've been a devotee for several years since.

When Puckette speaks of punch-downs as "delicate," she compares them to pump-overs, a more aggressive method of extraction that involves pumping wine up from the bottom of the tank—some-times using a large industrial hose-like tool—and splashing it over the top of the fermenting must.

What I experienced was officially not delicate.

Punch-downs are typically done by hand. They're popular among non-interventionist winemakers because they don't extract too much from the skins and add very little additional oxygen in the fermentation. To do punch-downs, you need a six-foot-tall tool that looks like a stainless steel pogo-stick. But instead of footrests for jumping, at the very bottom is a flat disc about a foot in diam-eter. (Also, you don't stand on the disc. Just to be clear.)

I'd seen Aaron use one before.
The process looked simple enough.

It was my turn now.

Aaron handed over the tool. I looked at the cap. I breathed in the yeasty, fruity aroma of the fermenting must and felt the heat of the carbon dioxide gas release into the air. I gripped the T-bar handle at the top and lowered the base into the tank. I started "delicately" plunging away at the cap—that thick layer of skins, stems and seeds that sits on top of the juice.

I submerged the tool again and again, breaking up the cap, stirring it into the juice. I did this all the way around three tanks. It was some of the hardest physical work I've ever done in my life.

As it happens, I'm writing this the day after another round or two of punch-downs. My triceps, biceps and shoulders are still screaming, *What on earth have you done to us?!*

(In case it's not obvious by now, "the big crush" does not refer to an object of adolescent affection. Quite the opposite. The big crush is the harvest. When the romance of winemaking can die.)

The caps in those tanks of Pinot Noir were tough and resistant. They had absolutely no desire to be broken up and submerged. Truth is, I didn't want to break them up either. Especially the second time. I had felt enough punch-down pain to know that this was going to hurt. I was resisting the resistance. I wanted someone else to do it. Anyone but me. Please.

And yet, other parts of my life have taught me that there is such a thing as good pain. That a kind of beauty exists in sacrifice and self-giving. That loss and grief have the potential to change and transform us, to make us more resilient, more courageous, more open, and present to others.

I have zero doubt that you've experienced this. We've all suffered, to one degree or another, and lived to tell about it. A worldwide pandemic, for example. We all have our Covid-19 stories to tell.

The theme of nearly every sports movie ever made is to face and overcome obstacles. A cardinal rule of good storytelling is that a protagonist has to encounter some sort of conflict. Writers sometimes call this an inciting incident: something they want but can't get unless they are willing to run a gauntlet they know will cause pain, create conflict, or cost something.

As Kelly Clarkson put it: *What doesn't kill you makes you stronger.*

On one level, this theme is low-hanging fruit. (I told you about the puns.) Yet I have to wonder why we keep coming back to it. Why are we drawn to the same plotline over and over again? Why do we feel so dependent on stories like these?

Sometimes, depending on what we're experiencing, it's a comfort to remember that even if things aren't okay, at some point they will be okay. Sometimes we simply forget the plot.

We need to be reminded that the very stories we're drawn to—the ones we've heard a million times, that have an inciting incident, plus trials and tribulations a-plenty—end in a denouement.

We need the wisdom of the mystics to encircle us. Like Julian of Norwich, who said, famously: *All shall be well, and all shall be well. And all manner of things shall be well.*

Somehow, we need to remember that every round of bicep-busting punch-downs is a necessary part of the pathway to gorgeous Pinot Noir.

When things are especially painful or difficult, and they've been that way a long time, it's easy to buy into the narrative that it will always be this way. To give in to despair. To resign. When you are suffering, it's a huge gift to hear, read, or watch someone else's story. To witness another human being hold onto hope amid struggle. To know we're not alone. We need their story because they mirror our story. They help us find places of belonging and connection. They remind us what it means to be human.

Allow me to tell you a bit of my own story in the hope that you'll find a bit of your own within it.

As I write, I'm grieving. It began when I learned that a dear friend—my closest male friend, who also happened to be my closest work colleague—was going to resign from the church where we both pastored. The church we started together ten years prior.

I understood his reasons. They made a lot of sense. I don't begrudge him leaving, and our friendship remains solid and growing. But now, things are different. After ten years working shoulder to shoulder, sharing some of the most significant challenges and joys, my good pal wasn't going to be my colleague anymore. It's been hard. It's been hard for him too, even though it was his choice to leave.

You don't get over that quickly. We built this thing together and his time was done. Now, I was to continue to build, but not with him.

I shared my struggle and some tears with a friend who is a really good listener. This friend is a treasure and also happens to be a spiritual director and a vocational coach.

She said, "It sounds to me like some of what you've lost is the intimacy of co-creation."
I shared more tears and said, "Yes, that's exactly what it's like."

Around this same time, our little family was moving to a new home in a different part of Vancouver. We left Yaletown—which is downtown, steps from the waters of False Creek—and moved to Mount Pleasant—which is uptown. Another goodbye, this one to a neighbourhood we loved and enjoyed and would greatly miss.

I also began to lose my previously consistent rhythm of running as exercise. In the five years prior, I ran five half-marathons. In preparation for those, I'd run anywhere between five and twenty kilometres, two or three times a week. All those runs happened on the seawall that circles the downtown core. Vancouver's seawall is, quite simply, one of the most beautiful settings on the planet for distance running. And we didn't live steps away from it anymore. Once we moved out of downtown, my running rhythms dwindled from two or three times a week, to once or twice a month.

It didn't take long before my grief began to intersect with that of others in some significant ways. And it wasn't just little deaths. There were big ones.

In February 2020, a young woman whose wedding I had offici-ated some years before died by suicide. She was someone who always lit up a room with her smile and whose laugh was nothing short of contagious. In over ten years as a pastor, it was the first time I hosted a Celebration of Life. I was heartbroken, to say the very least.

A month after that, Covid-19 hit. We plunged into what my friend Julia called *an ever-expanding interim.*

Author and essayist Zadie Smith called it the global humbling.[6]

Indeed.

The pandemic that began early in 2020 ushered the entire human race into a grieving process. So I don't want to be too precious about my own story. But neither do I want to shy away from telling it.

For my family, Covid meant that our daughter could no longer be in preschool three days a week. Which meant, among other things, a complete overhaul of our home and work rhythms, un-expected depths of physical tiredness and emotional exhaustion, marital and parental tensions, loss of mornings for writing, and less energy in general. Oh, and I can't forget this stellar pairing: a decreased motivation to exercise coupled with an increased motivation to eat Miss Vickie's chips.

On the work front, Covid meant that our church, which had been around for a decade, was somewhat back in start-up mode. We had to invent new ways to be a community and remain connected to one another. We had to learn how to keep rooted in our iden-tity as students and practitioners of the way of Jesus, to work for the good of our city, to attend to our emotional struggles, all from our living rooms, with our laptops, in our sweatpants. I know we weren't unique in this. Every single church, pastor, student, parent, child, business owner, employee—every living person has experienced loss at an unbelievable magnitude. The pandemic's harshest effect, of course, has been the loss of actual human life.

And while this pandemic has touched everyone, I'm reminded of a lesson I learned some years back. A lesson I need to keep re-learning all the time: everyone's story matters. Everyone's story deserves to be honoured. Including mine.

This lesson was driven deep, like a punch-down tool breaking through layers of inner resistance and obliviousness, when I was training to become a spiritual director.

Our facilitators assigned a writing exercise, inviting us to recount specific aspects of our stories: my *gifted* history, my *suffering* history, and my *shadow* history. For the part about suffering, I wrote this:

> *I don't often think of myself as one who has undergone a lot*
> *of suffering, particularly when I compare myself to others who*

have suffered a lot more than me. It occurs to me now that some of my resistance to this part of the assignment has been a desire to minimize my own experience of suffering. I think of myself as a compassionate person, but often feel as though that has been borne by walking alongside other people in their suffering, not something that has emerged from my own experience. I tend to think that 'other people always have it worse than I do'. Perhaps this is a subconscious attempt on the part of my false self to try to deny, diminish or 'live above' my own experience of suffering—like some kind of Stoic. Okay, that's probably something worth paying attention to!

My suffering matters.
Your suffering matters.
Don't minimize it.

These things we do—when we compare, when we place suffering on some sort of hierarchy, when we say *surely* this counts as suffering, but that *doesn't*—these things serve no one. That perspective doesn't shape us well, and it does nothing to help develop our empathy muscles.

Here's what I'm learning: as we attend to our own suffering, as we name it for what it is and allow ourselves to feel it, we begin to carve out the spaciousness that allows someone else to feel, name, and experience theirs as well.

One reason I wanted to share this part of my story is that at the present moment, it remains unresolved. The grieving process isn't over, and I have no idea when it will be. And I'm not even sure that over is the best way to talk about a grief process.[7]

I can tell you that I am not as afraid of grief as I once was. I can also say that I have grieved well. Part of the reason for this is that I have committed myself to locate my story inside another story.

At the epicentre of my faith tradition stands a symbol of torture, execution, and a crucified God. The cross event is a strange paradox. It was an unjust execution: cruel, brutal, and humiliating. Yet the victim, Jesus the Christ—the one the biblical prophets called *a man of sorrows, familiar with suffering*—entered it willingly. He chose to die. Why? Because he knew there was meaning in his suffering. (Which is not to say there is meaning in all suffering. Read the book of Job.[8])

Jesus knew what his death would accomplish: a salvation that was not only individual but social. One of the early witnesses to the story said it this way:

> *For God was pleased to have all his fullness dwell in Jesus, and through him to reconcile to himself all things, whether things on earth or things in heaven, by making peace through his blood, shed on the cross.*[9]

All things. All. Without exception.
The scope of redemption, says the apostle, has no limit. None.

And yes, our trust is in a Divine Being who endured suffering and death willingly.

The writer of Hebrews put it this way:

> *Keep your eyes on Jesus, who both began and finished this race we're in. Study how he did it. Because he never lost sight of where he was headed—that exhilarating finish in and with God—he could put up with anything along the way: Cross, shame, whatever. And now he's there, in the place of honour, right alongside God. When you find yourselves flagging in your faith, go over that story again, item by item, that long litany of hostility he plowed through. That will shoot adrenaline into your souls!* [10]

That doesn't mean it won't hurt.

A grape doesn't begin its life asking to be crushed into wine. But grapes are living things. They have cells. They grow. Also, my daughter is presently in kindergarten, which often makes me feel younger than I actually am. So if you'll permit me some playful imagination here for a moment.

If a grape were sentient, and if it could see what it might become on the other side of the big crush...

If a cluster of grapes were capable of having any inkling of the transformative potential they hold...

If the Love-that-sustains-all-things-and-holds-all-things-together mysteriously took shape as a conscious will within a tiny bud and eventually developed the ability to speak, I wonder if it might say...

Okay, this is gonna hurt. Eff it. Let's do this.

How does a person grow thick enough skin to be genuinely willing to suffer? To choose to endure the inevitable and necessary punch-downs of life, despite the pain they cause, for the sake of what comes after. I wonder if the answer begins with an awareness that we are meant to live our lives on behalf of others—with hearts broken open, not broken apart.

Indeed, harvest is where the romance of winemaking can die. But every winemaker will tell you that it's all worthwhile—the hard work, the long hours, the pain coursing through your entire body—all of it. Their number one piece of advice to anyone considering a career in the wine industry remains: Work a harvest. Not just to see if you're really into it (versus just the idea of it), or to kill your idealism, but to deepen your devotion. As we know from all the stories, there's something about living through adversity and coming out the other side.

We've all experienced deaths, large and small.

> Covid grief.
> The end of a relationship.
> Change we didn't ask for.
> Seasons where the losses keep piling up.
> Suffering histories and painful presents.

But suffering doesn't only signify endings. It can also mean something new is being formed.

When Jesus was nearing his death, his closest friends struggled to come to terms with the impending reality of life without him. Do you know what he told them? He said, "In this world you will have trouble. But take heart! I have overcome the world."[11]

In other words, tough times are part of the gig.
But hang in there. Beauty, too, can come from this.

And you're not alone.

Another harvest has come and gone. The big crush is over. As we prepare to head into the cellar, I'll leave you with a poem and a few questions to reflect on.

FALL GARDEN

In fall
the garden is spent
having given its all.

Cucumber vines lie exhausted on the ground
Tomato plants list to one side
Cornstalks stand dignified and empty
Sunflower faces droop earthward,
shades of their former selves.

All that has not been claimed lies mouldering in the dirt—
a bruised tomato, a forsaken pepper...
                    a misshapen pumpkin, a trampled stalk of beans.
What came from the earth is returning
to the place from whence it came.

There is an intimacy here,
        in the fall garden,
                gazing at living things in their demise.
I want to avert my eyes, avoid this tender grief.
Is this life or is this death? I cannot tell.

Ah, but there is beauty here
        amid all this death and dying.
To have given one's self fully
at least once
that is the thing.

To have spent oneself in an explosion of colour
*   to have offered one's body for food,*
*   one's very soul for nourishment...*
It is an unseemly generosity,
beauty of another kind.

In fall
the garden says, "This is my life, given for you."
And we are fed.
—Ruth Haley Barton [12]

What feels like the big crush in your life right now? Or the many little crushings?

What new ground might the Divine be breaking open within you?

What is making it difficult to trust?

What do you desire for your life? What do you hope it produces?

CELLAR

CHAPTER FIVE

Winemaking as Mystery

Why does wine grip us? Perhaps because, far from being an answer, replete with a grade, wine is more a bottled question.

—Matt Kramer, *Making Sense of Wine*

Wine is a mystery that holds the promise of an explanation.

—Randall Grahm

When you were little, did you ever get to see the cockpit of an airplane?

I remember seeing one for the first time, going, *Whoa, this is where it all happens! Look at all the lights! What does that red button do?* That sense of childlike awe and wonder gets close to what I felt like during my time in the cellar at Nk'Mip—with the people responsible for making the wine.

My favourite days were the cellar days.

When I was there in 2018, the winemaking team at Nk'Mip Cellars consisted of three people: Randy, Justin, and Aaron. Randy Picton, who has recently retired, was the senior winemaker, a position he held since 2002. Randy oversaw the entire portfolio at Nk'Mip and was specifically in charge of the red wines. Justin Hall, a member of the Osoyoos Indian Band, oversaw white wines. Justin worked alongside Randy since 2003 and has now replaced him as estate winemaker. I spent the most time with Aaron Crey who, until early in 2021, was the cellar supervisor. Aaron has since become a winemaker, joining up with a new team of producers called Vintners Cove.[1] I learned a lot from these guys, and I hold deep respect and gratitude for each. We also had a lot of fun.

Because we can describe wine very simply—an alcoholic beverage made with fermented grape juice—there is a sense that winemaking is not all that complicated. To make wine, you combine yeast with the sugar in grape juice, which creates alcohol and carbon dioxide. Easy, right? Well...

To explain what happens in the making of wine is one thing.
To create wine people want to drink is quite another.

Winemaking is both an art and a science. It involves countless steps combined with great attention to detail at each one. At times, the process requires ridiculous amounts of physical labour. At others, you need tenacious patience. And, as I observed in Randy, the winemaker's skill set is highly specialized and diverse. To make wine of high quality, you need a combination of:

mechanical skills (to operate and fix the equipment)
scientific knowledge (to understand, test, adjust, and curate the various chemical processes)
organizational ability (to keep everything together)

You also need a developed, finely-tuned palate.

Four primary senses prompt our palates: sight, smell, feel (texture), and taste. Some people have an extra-special knack for tasting.[2] But for us average folk, it takes hours of practice to learn to engage and harmonize these senses at once. Fortunately, as it happens, tasting wine is pretty fun. (We'll talk more about that in future chapters.)

On top of all this, winemakers often play a role in marketing. To do that well, you need to be personable and relatable. You need to tell the story of the wine you're selling.

Since this is not a textbook, I am under no obligation, dear reader, to offer you an exhaustive play-by-play of what it takes to make wine. There are plenty of other books and tours to teach you that if you're so inclined. In this chapter, I would like to offer one small part of the winemaking process for which I was fortunate enough to get a front-row seat.

Most of us know that some wines are made from one kind of grape—known as *varieties* or *varietals*. Some are made from multiple kinds of grapes. Wines made from one grape variety are called single varietal. Wines made from more than one are known as blends.

But what you may not know is that even single varietal wines are often blended.

(Yep. This was news to me as well!)

One morning Randy asked Aaron and me to pull some Pinot Noir samples from oak barrels, where the wine had been aging for about a year. We were going to get to taste some soon-to-be-released Pinot Noir. I was so stoked. First off, I *really* like Pinot. Second, this isn't something everybody gets to do.

Aaron and I had to source enough containers for the samples. We used half-litre glass jars to observe both colour and viscosity (the thickness or texture of the liquid). We gathered and cleaned the jars and began the trek cellarward.

Feeling giddy, I gingerly carried the box of empty jars down several flights of stairs to the red wine room. I couldn't contain my first-time-seeing-the-cockpit-like joy.

"Dude, this is awesome," I said. "How often do you get to do this?"

Aaron laughed. "Well, barrel tasting happens all the time, mainly to ensure that no off-flavours are happening. But this kind of comprehensive, focused, comparative tasting is something that's only done two or three times, starting about six or seven months before racking the barrels."

A wee sidebar is in order here: Aaron mentioned off-flavours. What are those?

Off-flavours during aging can stem from a variety of sources. A common one is a spoilage yeast called *Brettanomyces,* often abbreviated as *Brett,* which can impart aromas like barnyard, Band-Aid, wet dog, and worse (vomit). Brett is impossible to control, which is a big reason barrel tasting needs to be frequent.

Interestingly, in small doses, some strains of Brett contribute a pleasing complexity to wine. Sommelier Max Coane compares Brett to distortion in music, saying, "Distortion isn't a bad thing; it's the amplification of certain natural frequencies. However, it can and does get overused. Nobody wants to drink a wine that tastes like Nine Inch Nails."[3]

We arrive at the bottom of the stairs and step into the cool, dimly lit, red wine room, where barrels are stacked four-high and ten-deep. There we locate the precious Pinot and start to draw samples. I tried to keep spills to a minimum as the red wine filled my jars.

The samples were all Pinot Noir, each harvested from a different block (or section) within the vineyard—from different sides of the row and aged in different kinds of French oak barrels. If you've ever been to a working wine cellar, you may have noticed that every barrel has a label on it. Those labels contain a shorthand that requires translation.

For example, at Nk'Mip:

"7PGN – new" means 2017 Pinot, block G, north side, aged in new oak.
"7PJS – old" refers to 2017 Pinot, block J, south side, aged in old oak.

Aaron and I pulled about a dozen barrel samples in all, labelling each jar prudently. (As you might imagine, being off by even one letter could have significant consequences.) Then we headed back upstairs, where I had the privilege of tasting the samples with Justin and Randy.

I want to tell you about that tasting. But first, let's pause to consider another question:

What is barrel aging anyway? And what does it do to the wine?

Barrel aging is the heart of the activity known as *élevage*, a French term that means "raising" or "upbringing." It's used to express what happens to the wine between fermentation and bottling. (Leave it to the French to find a word that links wine-aging to child-rearing!)

A wine's élevage can last from a few months to several years. During this time, a wine's flavours and other characteristics (such as colour and texture) slowly integrate and mature. And if you're using oak to age your wine, the barrels themselves add magic to this mysterious process. How so? Oak barrels—whether American or European—are made from staves: long pieces of oak wood, fitted tightly together with metal hoops. The barrels are toasted over a fire to light, medium, or dark level. New barrels with a light toast will result in vanilla and caramel notes, while a darker toast will impart smoky, roasted aromas.

Besides adding flavour, oak also changes the tannin structure of red wines. You know that drying sensation in your mouth when you drink red wine? Those are tannins. They come from four main sources: skins, seeds, stems, and wood barrels. Texture is a helpful way to think about tannin quality: silky, plush, velvety. "Grippy" describes a pleasing amount of tannins, noticeable but not overbearing. "Green" usually refers to tannins that are bitter and have an astringency that's less-than-pleasant. "Polished" or "elegant" tannins are fine-grained in texture, both detectable and enjoyable.

It's possible to anticipate what will generally happen to the wine over time, based on the age and toast level of the barrels, for example. But there's always a degree of mystery involved. You can't know exactly what the oak is doing to the wine until you taste it.

So. Why taste twelve different Pinots side-by-side when you're only twelve months into an eighteen-month aging process? For several reasons. We tasted to learn what was going on in the individual barrels—to see how time, combined with oak, impacted the aroma and flavour profiles, the tannin structure, and acidity. We tasted to see how the overall balance and complexity of the wine were coming along. Ultimately, we tasted to discern which elixir of samples would eventually create the best possible blend of Pinot Noir.

Three large red wine glasses sat there on the counter, one for Justin, one for Randy, and one for me. Justin poured a small amount of the first sample into each glass, maybe an ounce or two. We looked, swirled, sniffed, and sipped. We swished the wine around in our mouths to try to get a multi-layered sense of what was going on: aroma, taste, texture, structure, acidity—all the things. Then we each spat our sample into the sink nearby. I realized quickly that there would be no swallowing. When you're on the job and regularly tasting multiple samples, you learn the art of spitting.

Then Justin poured the next one and the next.

As we tasted our way through these different Pinots, the childlike wonder was always present. Who was I to be standing here, swirling, and sniffing samples right alongside Nk'Mip's winemaking team? Also, I was amazed at how these wines, each made from the same varietal, could have such subtle-yet-detectable differences.

My sense of wonder was paired with more than a little bit of intimidation. These guys were the pros. Their palates were miles ahead of mine in the art of tasting. After each sample, the two of them talked about it a bit. I was welcome to contribute, and occasionally I did, but mostly I listened.

Justin would be like, "Wow, the fruit in this one is really pronounced." Or Randy would say, "The tannins in this one are rounder than the first."

Some of their observations I noticed and could discern. Others I couldn't. But that was okay.

After we tasted them all, Randy went into his office and punched out four different Pinot Noir blend recipes, with varying percentages of each sample, based on what he was tasting. Two at a higher tier (which means a higher price point and overall quality), and two at a lower tier (a lower price point). Randy and Justin measured out the four blends and placed them at the centre of the table. And on either side, the two of them discussed which they liked the most and whether they wanted to take another crack at a different blend.

I felt so humbled to be part of that barrel tasting process, that single moment in time. It's something these winemakers do frequently, and for them, it perhaps gets routine or mundane. But I never got the sense that it felt like a chore to Randy or Justin, or worse, like a burden. It was something they took delight in, pride even. And they were fully engaged and attentive in the work. They even seemed humbled by it themselves, given all the variables and unknowns that are part of each vintage.

In one sense, this was just another day in the cellar, not a big deal. And yet, when a craftsperson is devoted to their craft, each step in the process becomes nothing less than an expression of love.

Now, whenever I open a special bottle to enjoy over dinner with family or friends, I try to do better and remember that wine is a living, changing organism. The long, slow transformation from grape to glass is deeply mysterious, not to mention miraculous. Barrel aging happens in the dark. Hidden from view. You can't understand how the wine is being refined and reshaped unless you pull out a sample, look at it, and taste it.

So there's a combination of trusting the élevage—allowing the wine to grow, mature, and change—and, at the same time, attending to what's happening, as we're able.

I think this snapshot of the winemaking process reveals a lot about what it means to be attuned to mystery.

In our lives, we don't always see what God is doing. Especially when it comes to the deeper places of our formation. We don't always know what the Love That Is The Ground Of All Being is up to. I'm slowly coming to learn that that's okay. We can trust the process because of Who's behind it. But, just like palate development, trust doesn't come naturally to most of us.

It is shocking that we casually refer to Christianity as a *faith* tradition, yet so often, when it comes to our daily lived experience, we default to walking by sight, not by faith. [4]

We would much rather see than not see. I'd rather know than not know.

My growing conviction is that we need a more robust spirituality of unknowing. We need to make friends with mystery. Gratefully, there are mystics and winemakers who show us the way. One truth I'm learning from both is that not knowing doesn't mean we're not growing. Just because I may not be able to tell you exactly how God is maturing me at a particular moment, doesn't mean nothing is happening. In fact, it's usually quite the opposite.

97

Our upbringing in God means surrendering to the invitation to trust that God's intentions are like those of a good winemaker. It may not look how we envision it. We won't be able to control every aspect of the process. Nor will it likely be on the timeline we'd prefer. But we can be confident that God longs to create something beautiful in and through our lives. We can entrust ourselves to Divine élevage.

Let's take a few moments to do a little contemplative exercise together.

Below is a quote from the late Cistercian monk and author, Father Thomas Keating. Read it aloud slowly, at least two times, more if you wish. Underline the image, word, or phrase that stands out to you. Then notice what you've noticed. See if there might be something along the lines of an invitation to you personally. I'll even give you a bit of space to jot a few notes down right here in the book.

When you've done that, continue reading, and I'll share a bit of how this wisdom lands with me. Sound good? Okay, go.

> The way of pure faith is to persevere in contemplative practice [any intentional activity that opens us to God, such as silence, meditation on Scripture, and other forms of contemplative prayer] without worrying about where we are on the journey, and without comparing ourselves with others or judging other's gifts as better than ours. We can be spared all this nonsense if we surrender ourselves to the divine action, whatever the psychological content of our prayer may be. In pure faith, the results are often hidden, even from those who are growing the most...The divine light of faith is totally available in the degree that we consent and surrender ourselves to its presence and action within.[5]

What resonated with you? Any invitations you noticed?

_____

_____

_____

_____

_____

_____

_____

_____

_____

_____

This is where I went in my mind and heart:

The idea of not worrying how I compare to others sounds liberating, because I'm prone to comparison. To be free of the compulsion to judge myself or others is an exciting prospect. I continue to feel invited to live into the freedom of non-comparison. And to notice how contemplative practice helps me do just that. But I'm not so sure I like the part about hidden results. I often feel caught up in the cultural tsunami where everything is geared toward success, achievement, and measurable goals. I mean, how will I know I'm getting the results I want unless I can tweet about them?

"Your transformation throughout life will be a paradox," wrote artist and author Scott Erickson in his book *Honest Advent*. "The choice to do daily sit-ups and refrain from cookies-and-cream milkshakes will create a transformation in your abdominal area. Gratitude and thankfulness are choices you can make to transform your perspective in every situation you find yourself in."[6]

As in life, so in winemaking. Winemakers decide when and how to ferment, age, and blend their wines. Similarly, you have agency in your transformation.

At the same time, parts of the journey remain a mystery. Aspects of being raised in God we have no control over. Off-flavours may well occur. You might lose your job. Meaningful relationships may end. A pandemic could hit.

How do we remain open to Mystery—to all that God wants to do in us and to the beauty God wants to create—when these things happen?

Go back to the Keating quote and notice the verbs there.

> Persevere.
> Practise.
> Surrender.
> Consent.

That's the better part of what I believe we are here for.
These aren't passive postures, but they do necessitate waiting and trusting.
They're action words, but that doesn't mean we'll look busy.

These verbs remind me that I am not the Prime Motivating Force in the universe. We are not the primary initiative-takers in the relationship, but God invites us to be agents in our becoming. How might we learn to participate in attunement to Mystery?

One of the many gifts of contemplative tradition is that it helps us stay engaged in the process of transformation through practices like Centring Prayer.

If you've never heard of it, I invite you to go to the App Store, type in "centring prayer" (it may be spelled "centering" because USA) and download the app. Read it. Follow the steps, make it as regular a practice as you're able. Entrust your spiritual upbringing to God.

If centring prayer is new to you, as it was to me not so long ago, you may find yourself asking: *Wait, how does this work again? I just sit there for 20 minutes? That's it? How does that count as prayer? Am I supposed to hear anything from God? Not necessarily? Okay, then what good is this actually supposed to do?*

If that's you, do not fear. You are not alone. My first spiritual director initially opened me up to the gift of silent and centring prayer. He gave me the following to pray, silently or audibly, before beginning a session.

> Holy Blessed Trinity, my Lord and my God,
> I firmly believe that you are here,
> That you see me, that you hear me, that you know me,
> that you love me and that by your choice I am yours.
> I love you, sometimes hesitantly, oftentimes haltingly,
> yet very deeply. I humbly accept your pardon for my sin.
> And in these moments of silence set aside with you,
> I ask for the courage and the grace
> to be open to the transforming action
> of your unconditional love.

Being silently open to the transforming action of Love is not the same thing as doing nothing. I found this helpful when I first started. I return to this prayer on occasion, in times I feel unhealthy and unsure of myself, or if I've been unwilling or unable to pray for a time. For me, this prayer functions as an anchor, a True North that points to the why and the intent of centring prayer.

Consider giving yourself to this practice for a season. It will be hard, but I promise you will not be disappointed. Over time, notice what happens when, rather than hit the ground running every morning, you start the day with five-, ten- or 20-minutes opening to Love.

Notice less reaction and more response.

Notice less anxiety and more genuine presence to those around you.

Notice less obsession with knowing and more openness to the Mystery that surrounds. Safe, dark, hidden, like an oak barrel. A place for all the holy fermentation and graceful aging that Divine Love wants to affect in you.

Recognize that all of this is Grace.
Trust the Winemaker.
And give thanks.

CHAPTER SIX

Cellar Maintenance

I put one foot in front of the other today

I stretched my arms out wide and it felt real strange

And then my legs, they started shaking

And my hands, they started quaking

'Cause things just take longer to heal these days

—**Griff**, *One Foot In Front Of The Other*

It's a lot harder to find fault with the mundane details of daily existence when you really, really know on a cellular level that you're going to go, and that this moment, right now, is life. Life isn't what happens to you in twenty years. This moment, right now, is your life.

—**Alan Ball**

You know those times when you're not doing super well, but you're also not doing horribly? Times when it would be nice to have something impressive (or even interesting) to talk about: a project you're working on, a new hobby or pursuit—even something you're looking forward to—but life just feels uninteresting, typical, mundane, and boring.

When I'm stuck in seasons like these, I think of myself as being in a sort of maintenance mode. I may be going through a serious and seemingly unending case of the blahs, but I still want to live the life I've been given.

It's important to keep going.

When we're in maintenance mode, we tend to think we're not really thriving but still surviving. Maybe we've experienced a recent setback, such as losing a job, or something more serious like a failed relationship, or the death of someone close to us, or the year two thousand and twenty.[1]

What does putting one foot in front of the other look like when we're in maintenance mode? It depends.

Consider other words that carry similar meanings. To maintain is to *keep up, preserve, sustain, or nurture.* These actions can take different forms. Let me offer a few quick thoughts on each.

KEEP UP

For me, keeping up often means rest. It's an action that looks precisely like inaction. To keep up my physical, emotional, spiritual, and mental health, I need to take breaks. We are not the Energizer bunny. Our batteries run out and we need to recharge. Rest is a vital part of maintenance mode.

PRESERVE

When I think of this word, I hear my Dad drilling into me the importance of getting regular oil changes "to preserve the life of your car." We preserve mouth health by going to the dentist every six months (or if you're a sub-par flosser like me, every four). It's spending time and money on things we don't necessarily enjoy because we want our lives to last—both for our sake and for those we love.

SUSTAIN

Do y'all know what a sustain pedal is? It's that magical foot pedal every piano has, where, when you press it, anything you play gets held a little longer. A sustained note. A sustainable pace. Sustainable practices. What a beautiful word. I love the idea of maintenance mode being a place you get to be held a little longer. (Which begs the question, who's holding you?)

NURTURE

Nurture can, of course, look like different things to different people. I can't help but think of nurture through the lens of parenting. Recently, on a rainy Saturday afternoon, I was relaxing with my daughter, snuggled together on the couch, enjoying a show she had recently discovered. It was raining cats and dogs outside, but we were warm, cozy, and safe inside. A short while later, it was time for dinner. For various reasons, our precious Adri had a hard time listening and refused to come to the table. Emotions were high and hot, we yelled at each other (for which we apologized later), and there was a time-out (again, something we both needed).

Both scenarios fall squarely under the heading of nurture. There are times when nurture looks like coziness on the couch, requiring nothing but the will to stay put and be close. And there are times when it feels more like a time-out, requiring every ounce of emotional energy we can muster.

The point? Maintenance mode can look vastly different, but it all matters. It all belongs. Recognizing this can help us tolerate, even celebrate, the mundane in our own lives. At the same time, it can go a long way to help build our empathy muscles.

Think about when you texted someone and they didn't reply within your expected, hallowed, and holy timeline. Have you ever considered the countless other tasks the other person might be saying yes to while they're not responding to you? And might those other things—their kids, their job, their rhythms of self-care—be worthy of periodic seasons of scheduled maintenance? They'd better be.

What if we could reimagine maintenance mode as something alive with potential? As a mode that deserves pride of place within The Growing Season? What would it be like to consider "scheduled maintenance" an active part of our real, ordinary, and precious lives instead of a period of latency, where we twiddle our thumbs and wait for something extraordinary to happen?

Much of the winegrowing season—both in the vineyard and the cellar—is spent in maintenance mode. It's maybe not the most exciting time. Things get boring. But it's absolutely necessary.

If a winemaker uses oak barrels to age their wine, then a good portion of cellar maintenance falls under the broad category of *barrel work*. From choosing origins and styles of oak, to cleaning the barrels after an aging season is over, cellar hands spend a ton of their time with these beautiful, practical, painstakingly crafted containers of precious liquid cargo.

In the few days I spent in the cellar, I learned a few basics of barrel work. One is known as *topping barrels*. This is the process of refilling (or topping) wine that has evaporated. Over time, since barrels aren't entirely airtight, evaporation increases what's known as ullage, the headspace of air between the wine and the top of the barrel. The rate of evaporation varies due to temperature, relative humidity, the movement of air in the cellar, and the integrity of the barrel. If you're fortunate enough to be aging your wine in a subterranean cave where the air is naturally cool, humid, and motionless, you will have less evaporation than you'd find in a dry, breezy space with air-conditioning. Most winemakers aren't so lucky, however. They need to top their barrels anywhere from every couple of days to every few weeks.[2] So, to avoid spoilage caused by bacteria and to reduce the wine's exposure to air (which can mean oxidized notes and further evaporation), winemakers fill the headspace. They top the barrels using wine that has been set aside in anticipation of evaporation.

If winemakers want to nurture a top-quality product, it's vital that they top their barrels regularly. Topping is a necessary part of good cellar maintenance.

Nk'mip Cellars produces about 18,000 cases annually. At peak capacity, they're aging between seven and eight hundred barrels, which can take up to two days to top. This happens every month.

I helped Aaron, the cellar supervisor, top barrels one day. I've gotta say, there's an art to it. For one thing, wine barrels are not small. You've likely seen them before. And they're heavy. A typical oak barrel weighs about 600 pounds, to which you add 60 gallons of wine. Barrels also take up a lot of space. Since cellars don't have endless square footage, they get stacked up on racks. At Nk'Mip, they're stacked as many as four barrels high, or about 13 feet tall, which is about the same height as a regulation basketball backboard. So if you're topping the barrels on the top row, it's like you're standing on the rim—ten feet off the ground. For some, this is not an extreme altitude. But if you're like me, and you don't enjoy close friendship with heights, you may as well be standing on a window ledge outside a skyscraper.

There are fears to be overcome, even when you're in maintenance mode.

The topping process itself, though unexciting, requires meticulous attention to detail. First, you need to pull wine from containers that store sub-barrel volumes, known as breakdown vessels. These containers can be big—like the 15-gallon kegs behind the bar at your local pub—or small, like a big 'ol jug of moonshine from an old Western movie. These smaller glass "carboys" usually hold one to five gallons of wine.

And of course, you want to top *like with like*. For example, you top your finest Merlot with your finest Merlot whenever possible. If a winemaker doesn't have a breakdown of a particular variety, most will top with a similar or compatible wine. (Using a carboy of Chardonnay—a white grape—to top Cabernet Sauvignon—a red grape—is, generally speaking, not advisable.)

Once you've got your desired topping wine ready to go, the mechanics are quite efficient. In our case, we transferred the wine into a 15-gallon keg. Then we attached a topping rig (a long hose with a trigger valve) on one end and a high-pressure nitrogen cylinder to the other. This pressurizes the keg with nitrogen, an inert gas that prevents the wine from being exposed to oxygen during the topping process. The long hose let us hop from barrel to barrel to top each one off quickly. By "us," I mean Aaron. He hopped around, nimble and surefooted as a mountain goat. I, by contrast, moved slowly and cautiously among the barrels, like whatever is the most nervously timid kind of animal.

I spent a grand total of three hours doing something Aaron does for two days every single month of the year. So for me, it was admittedly a bit of a novelty. Aaron has to do it. I got to do it. Even though I made small mistakes and was slow, it was legit fun for a couple of hours. For a short window of time, the boredom slowed me down enough to awaken curiosity. I wonder, though, if that could be sustained. I'm not sure I'd get too excited about spending the equivalent of three weeks out of every year topping barrels. Then again, does the universe owe me 24/7 excitement?

Winemaking is just one of many tasks that reminds me that, on some level, I need to learn to normalize boredom. The truth is, without consistent and diligent attention to seemingly ordinary details, great wine would not get made. When I look at it that way, I think, *This is a no-brainer. Great wine is worth my occasional boredom.*

Maintenance is attendance.

It's keeping up by topping up.
It's sustenance, preservation, and nurture.

All of which can feel mind-numbing.

Having said that, as routine as maintenance mode might be, there are ways to make it less boring and more life-giving. In times of health, we tend to remember those ways and seek them out. It's often when we're stressed or busy that we tend to complain about the mundanity of our lives.

One constant in my life's mundane moments is music. I know I'm not alone in this. Music is a universal companion to boredom.

What do we do the second after we turn the ignition in our cars, hop on the bus, or hit the sidewalk? We put some music on.

When we're in the gym or on a run, our preferred albums and playlists keep us company through our earbuds.

When we wash the car or the dishes, or clean the garage or the bathroom, music is like a friend we rarely tire of.

When I was nine, my Dad was a pastor in a young church that didn't have an administrator. So it fell to my brother Chris and me to fold the bulletins for Sunday morning worship. It became a Saturday afternoon ritual.

A stack of 150 printed-yet-unfolded legal-size bulletins waited for us at the dining room table. Next to that was a stack or two of half-page inserts (our groaning at the monotony of our task increased correlative to the number of inserts). The two of us, still in our PJs, arranged our official folding stations.

"Mom," we'd call out, "can we have a snack?" She'd bring us some Ritz crackers, cheese, and juice. Or tell us to get it ourselves.

The last step before we started was to pick a favourite record.

Now. I know many of you reading this—at least those who grew up in a North American evangelical Christian subculture—are desperately interested in what those favourite records would have been. So I'm going to tell you. If that wasn't your background, just go ahead and skip the next few paragraphs. I won't be offended because I won't know.

One was "Mansion Builder," the 1978 recording by *2nd Chapter of Acts*.

Then came "A Song in the Night" by *Silverwind*, an ABBA-esque Christian supergroup with tight harmonies and catchy melodies in spades. To this day, if either Silverwind or The Bulletin Folding Era comes up in a conversation with my brother, he will inevitably start singing the line, "Sheeeee likes to eat cotton candy," and I'll continue with "And take walks through the park or the zoo." And then together, "And play games like all children do...Destiny." (The song is "Destiny" by Silverwind. If you've never heard it, you are missing out. Worth a YouTube search.)

And then *Michael W. Smith Project* came out in 1983. That was the moment when folding bulletins officially became the high point of our week. I'm sure we wore the grooves off that record.

In that season, music became a sacred gift, infusing an otherwise humdrum Saturday afternoon with singing, laughter, and memories. Music has been such a gift many, many more times since. Like the summers I spent earning extra cash helping my brother do drywall. We always had the radio going on the jobsite. And we always sang along. If we didn't know the words, we'd make them up. Other tradespeople didn't know what to do with these weirdos who kept singing all day. Sometimes, though, they'd join us. I mean, if you're on a jobsite and "Roxanne" comes on and you're not singing, *you're* the weirdo.

Like other art forms, music helps us imbue the banal with meaning. It has a knack for winding its way into our souls. Music slows us down. It beckons us toward wonder and curiosity. Sometimes it even makes us forget we've just spent an hour folding bulletins.

If you'll permit a quick jaunt back out to the vineyard, I want to reflect briefly on maintenance mode in that setting.

Some gardeners insist that talking to their plants makes a difference in how they grow. The Queen of Burgundy, Lalou Bize-Leroy, speaks of loving her vines— being part of both their life, and the life of the soil. Pregnant mothers often listen to music, believing it can have a positive impact on the character of their baby.

Similarly, there are some who think music can play a role in helping wine age well.

Thibault Morey, the winemaker at Domaine Morey-Coffinet, says in the film A Year in Burgundy, "Since these cellars were constructed by the Cistercian monks back in the 16th century... there's a special atmosphere down here. I love it. Often, I put on some classical music in the barrel room. It does me good, and I think it does the wine good too. Wine is alive. From the moment you pick the grapes till the moment you drink it, it's alive. Music calms it as it matures."

Does classical music do wine any good, as Thibault claims? Would the wine turn out the same whether the fermenting grape juice heard music frequently or not?

I'm not aware of a scientific study that would prove (or disprove) such a hypothesis. But I've known, and am continually rediscovering, the ways music does me good. And of course, when I'm doing alright, that health has a spillover effect on the rest of my life: my parenting, my relationships, my work.

One more question, for those feeling the mystery/soul vibes, before we return to the cellar: *If we imagine God as winemaker, how might God be singing to us when we're in maintenance mode?*

On the day Aaron and I topped barrels, we talked music. He had a few friends over the night before to share some food, wine, and conversation, during which they listened to some big band jazz. They had a great time. He remembered how much he enjoyed listening to jazz and wondered aloud why he didn't do it more often. I'm sure we could all make mental lists of activities we know enhance our lives, but for myriad reasons, we don't engage them.

We were about to start topping another row of Merlot when he said, "What kind of jazz do you like? Do you listen to much big band?"

Jazz is a deep passion of mine. I play it, listen to it, and I also love to talk about it. So the question itself lifted me above the ordinary.

I said, "Most of the big band stuff I listen to has a singer as well, like Ella Fitzgerald or Sarah Vaughan. Or Frank Sinatra."
"Oooh, I like Sinatra," Aaron said. "You know what? We've got some speakers in this room. I sometimes put on music down here."
"Nice! I'd love to listen to something."

He pulled out his phone and connected the Bluetooth.
"What's your favourite Sinatra album?"
"Sinatra at the Sands," I said. "It's a live album, recorded in Vegas. The Count Basie orchestra backs him up. It's amazing."
"Let's put it on!"
"Sounds good to me!"

So we topped barrels and listened to Sinatra. Which was followed by Miles Davis' *Kind of Blue*, arguably the greatest jazz album of all time.

I thought to myself, *This has to be maintenance mode at its best.*

I invite you to join me in raising a glass in praise of maintenance mode.
Non-sexy.
Boring.
Mundane.
Lonely.

And completely necessary for human flourishing.
Something to welcome, not avoid. May we learn to do maintenance mode better.

Holy cheers.

BOTTLE

CHAPTER SEVEN

Pairings

Earth's crammed with heaven,

And every common bush afire with God;

But only he who sees, takes off his shoes,

The rest sit round it and pluck blackberries.

—Elizabeth Barrett Browning

Sometimes you have to watch somebody love

something before you can love it yourself.

It is as if they are showing you the way.

—Donald Miller

When I think of my favourite moments and experiences where wine is involved, I realize that the enjoyment is never just about the wine itself. It's about what goes with it. In any friendship, you have things in common. Shared affections that help strengthen ties and thicken bonds. As I've said already, my love of wine was born in friendship. Pam and Chad Teigen are dear friends who live in Canada's Wine Capital (Oliver, BC).

One thing my wife and I had in common with the Teigens was tasting wine.

When we first started making trips to see our friends, in the years before our daughter entered our lives, we developed a wine tasting rhythm that we joyfully replicated several times over. That infectious rhythm? Four wineries in a day. Two in the late morning, followed by a lunch break (preferably in a bistro at the second winery), then two more in the afternoon. We'd seek out wineries that were near each other, both to minimize the time for travel and to maximize the time for savouring the magical pairing of wine and friendship.

In those days, you didn't need to book ahead. You'd just rock up to the counter and be greeted by one of the loveliest questions in existence:

"Are you here for a tasting?"

(*Yes, please.*)

We'd choose a specific area, like one of the Okanagan's official sub-regions—Golden Mile Bench, Naramata Bench, Okanagan Falls, or Skaha Bench—and map out our four visits. Either Pam or Chad would volunteer to be the designated driver. (They were both generous and responsible hosts.)

When the day arrived, we'd pile in the car like carefree children and venture forth to Winery No. 1. We'd listen to Coldplay, because they were undeniably cool back then (just like we were). We'd sing, laugh, and swap stories. We'd nerd out about wine, whether we knew what we were talking about or not. Our palates slowly developed as we learned what we liked and what we didn't. We'd purchase a favourite bottle or two from each winery. Our annual wine budget began to grow.

By the end of the day, there was this feeling.

Wow, that was fun.

A feeling that, quite honestly, reminded me of my daughter's sense of wonder and her unbridled desire to, say, keep being pushed on a swing:

Again!
Again, Mama!
Do it again!

What was it about the experience that made it so enjoyable? The company, of course, was a big part of it. It was who we were with: shared history among dear friends. We supported each other through some rough times. Got lost in Venice together (which, for the record, was one hundred percent not my fault). Got stranded on the tarmac at London's Heathrow Airport in the wake of a bomb scare. Loved each other through various episodes of family drama (and trauma).

But our shared history doesn't just include the difficult things. We share joys as well. Watching Star Wars together while wearing track pants and eating popcorn and M&Ms. Seeing Les Mis in London's West End. Watching our kids grow up. And touring wineries.

Enduring friendships enhance the pleasure of wine tasting.
It's a pairing you can always count on.

And it's not just old friends who do this. New connections can bring a different kind of enjoyment, brief as they may be. Like those little interactions that happen when you turn up to a tasting room. Sometimes, when it's not too busy and there's no lineup, the host engages you as human rather than customer—they take a minute to ask, "Where are you from?"—and you connect on another level. Has this happened to you? It's beautiful, for example, when the staff speak knowingly and lovingly about other wineries and the wines they produce. When they think of themselves not just as competitors, but colleagues. And if the host notices I'm entering the tasting with a posture of openness and appreciation, the possibility for mutual admiration and enjoyment increases all the more.

Wine pairs well with old friends and new connections.
It also goes great alongside learning and growth.

One afternoon I was working the harvest at Nk'Mip. Randy, who was the senior winemaker, gathered the cellar team to close out the day with a little blind tasting. One white, one red. Nothing super fancy or elaborate. Just some time to come together for a break and some fun. Even though it wasn't that big a deal, I felt out of my depth. I shuffled my feet, put my hands in my pockets and fidgeted with my keys, laughed a bit too loudly at whatever Randy was saying when he poured the wine. I immediately positioned myself on the lowest rung of an imagined hierarchy called Palate Expertise.

I had two thoughts.

One (more like a prayer): *Please help me not look like an idiot.*
Two (this one even surprised me): *Bring it on. There is nothing at*

stake here besides my ego. I've got some game as a taster, and my palate is getting better all the time. Maybe I'll do ok.

Randy poured the white. I looked at it intently, swirled it in my glass and gave it a good sniff. (We're going to talk about why that's important in another chapter, by the way. And why people who swirl their wine aren't just trying to be fancy.)

I did it again. Look. Swirl. Sniff. Sip.

My palate told me, This is Pinot Gris. I'm almost positive. Then we were invited to guess the varietal. I was too nervous to speak first, so I waited for someone else to say something. I don't recall what the first guess was, but it wasn't Pinot Gris.

Internal dialogue:

Shit. Yeah. I'm probably wrong.
Do I say it anyway?
If I do and I'm wrong, I'll look silly.
On the other hand, if I say it and I'm right, well...

"Pinot Gris?" I blurted out.

Then someone else echoed my guess and, suddenly, I didn't feel so alone. *Okay. This is okay.*

As it turned out, I was right.

And not to brag, but I was right about the red, too, even though I had a couple of misguided wonderings at first. Sometimes you need to travel down a few wrong paths before you land on the right one. It's not the end of the world. And you know what? If I'd said the wrong answer, it wouldn't have been the end of the world either. I suspect that's not news to many of you. But for some reason, it's taken a while for me to clue into that fact.

If there's a lesson I need to learn on the regular, it's this: There are worse things than being wrong.

Every wine tasting is an opportunity to learn.

As you look at, swirl, sniff, and sip your wine, pay attention to what you notice. Swirl and sip again. Pick up on aromas you missed before. The more often you do this, the more confidence you develop in your palate. And the higher the possibility that you just might pick up on something the experts missed.

As I recount this story and others like it, I realize that tasting wine has played a role in my ability to stand in my truth. To find my voice. To risk being wrong.

Maybe it's not wine tasting for you. Then again, you are reading this book! But something entirely different may evoke that sense of deep delight in you. Something you never seem to tire of learning about. Something that, like an infectious melody, simply sticks in your brain and won't let up.

Take a moment right now to reflect. You don't have to name *the* thing. Just try to name *something*. A passion. A pursuit. A hobby. A love.

How have you been shaped in the process of learning more about what you love?

Let me be clear. As I've been saying since page one, I enjoy wine for wine's sake. But wine, as it turns out, pairs well with many other growth curves in my life. It was fun, even gratifying, to be right about a blind tasting. But far more important was that

I fought through the false narratives that confined me to my petty fears.

Fears of looking like an idiot and being wrong.
Of appearing less-than.
That low-grade anxiety that compares myself to others.
Thinking of myself as inferior and unworthy of attention or respect.

At least in that single, bright, shimmering moment, I found the courage to rewrite one of the scripts I'd been rehearsing and began to live into a new one.

Here's another key to this learning: Not only did I rewrite the script. I noticed that I did.
The other day, my wife Terri said, "I think Adri grew last week."
"Yeah, you're probably right," I said. "Let's go check."

We went straight to her room, where we have a growth chart with jungle animals on it. We measured her up and sure enough.
"Adri, you're halfway up the crocodile tail now!"

How do you picture your own inner growth chart?
How tall is your confidence these days? Are your fears shrinking (even a little bit)?
What are the practices that help you notice, name, and own the fact that you're growing?

So, it was in the context of wine tasting, of all things, that I found my voice. I noticed what it was saying. I also gave it a name and then I spoke that name into being. In other words, I remembered the story and somehow found the courage to tell it.

Do you have stories you'd like to tell, but something's holding you back?

One of my dearest friends happens to be one of the world's greatest storytellers. His name is Lance. For one thing, he has an uncanny ability to *remember* stories. A big reason for that is that he's lived through some pretty crazy ones. He's always ready to share, and seldom does one listen to his stories and not end up either reaching for the tissues or ROFLing.[1] He knows how to take you to the heights and depths of your emotional landscape.

I love a Lance story. And so does everyone else.

Problem was, we weren't just friends. We were colleagues for over ten years. Lance was a preacher in the same church where I preached. So. There I am: prone to compare myself to others, especially those in a similar role. It was a constant inner battle.

When Lance told a story on a Sunday morning, I would look around at everyone, and they'd be completely rapt with attention. For the longest time, it was hard to appreciate those stories for what they were—and for what my friends and fellow congregants received from them—without rehearsing the script: *Lance is such a phenomenal storyteller. I'll never be able to tell stories like him. He's in a league of his own.*

Theodore Roosevelt is often attributed with the saying, "Comparison is the thief of joy." Oof. Boy, I've come to know that firsthand.

But here's another oft-repeated sentiment: *The first step is knowing you have a problem.*

Constant comparison was my problem. I'd known it for a good while. Once I named it, it started to loosen its grip on my sense of identity. Lance has known about my inner journey of comparison for years. And I know his. We talked about it often when we worked together. And we both grew in not comparing ourselves to others, and to each other in particular. (Incidentally, Lance's ceaseless encouragement to tell my own stories is one of the biggest reasons this book exists.)

So, I want to ask you: Who or what do you compare yourself to? How might it look to trust your voice and tell your stories?

In this chapter, we've talked about how wine pairs with friendship, as well as with learning and growth. I've shared a few of my own stories along those lines and invited you to reflect on yours. Remember how, in the Introduction, I said we'd take some side roads because the spiritual journey isn't always linear? If it wasn't clear by now, that's what's going on here. Before we open a new chapter, though, there's one more pairing I want to talk about.

Wine tasting as a spiritual practice.

There. I said it.
I believe an intentional practice of focused wine tasting can form the soul in some deep, fruitful, beautiful ways.

You might be thinking: *Well, that's a bit of a leap, isn't it? Drinking alcoholic beverages in the name of growth as a follower of Jesus?*

That's fine. You have every right to think that. But stay with me.

How can wine tasting be a spiritual practice?

Well, tasting wine is a **singular** activity.

Think about all the things we do that aren't singular. When you drive a car, you're doing one thing. It's singular. When you listen to music as you drive, that's two things. When you talk to someone in the passenger seat, as music plays in the background while you drive, now you're up to three. We human beings are notorious multi-taskers. And quite often, we forget how to do just one thing. Like how to have a conversation with a friend across the dinner table without checking your phone.

We need to re-learn how to do one thing. To recognize and acknowledge we have limits. Which in turn, helps us realize our need for others, for love, and to be continually grounded in God.

And again, I'm talking about *intentional* tasting. Not throwing your leftover Apothic Red into a thermos, so you can sneak it to a picnic, to pour into Solo cups and pair with egg salad sandwiches. I'm talking about focused tasting. To notice the wine's unique characteristics that distinguish it from another. To learn how the wine reflects its terroir—its somewhereness. To allow such learning to deepen your appreciation.

Wine Tasting as Spiritual Practice (should I be ™ing this?) can happen in a tasting room, at a wine club, or any occasion that is about discovering, appreciating, and comparing a series (or "flight") of wines. Sitting down to enjoy wine with a meal can be a spiritual practice, too (we've all seen *Babette's Feast,* right?), but it's not singular in the same way.

And please don't get me wrong. If you haven't gleaned this by now, I believe there is definitely a place for the mere enjoyment of wine. There must be. Terry Theise said, "I know full well that wine can be important, that it can be an embodiment of culture, that it can be a messenger of meaning, a portal into the mystery. But if wine must always be solemnly Important, then life gets pretty dour."[2]

The next time you visit a winery, do your best to notice and appreciate the singularity of what you're doing. And then—here's where you begin to see what's happening beneath the surface of your life—pay attention to how you show up in one-thingness:

Is it hard to focus on just tasting wine?

If so, why do you think that is?

How strong is the compulsion to do an additional thing, like posting "Apples and peaches and pears, oh my!" while boomeranging your sweet swirling action on Instagram?

What would it be like to go into a tasting room and leave your phone behind?
Could you do it?

What was your reaction even to reading that sentence?

If it feels like I'm trying to do spiritual direction through the words on this page, then you're reading it right. Go with me one level deeper.

If you ask yourself these questions, can you answer honestly and without judgment?

Can you exercise self-compassion and recognize you're not weird because you feel a magnetic pull to multitask in a tasting room?

Are you able to appreciate that you are loved, and infinitely worthy of love, even though these compulsions may take up more space than you'd like in your inner world?

This seems to be a good moment to say, as tenderly and personally as I'm able through the printed page, that your compulsions, misplaced affections, and attachments are not the sum total of who you are. You may feel like they're most obvious to everyone around you. But I assure you, they're not.

There's an illustration by Scott Erickson that spoke profoundly to me on this theme.

The image is of a jeep with a cracked windshield, and the caption reads: "May I never consider my weaknesses and faults the larger or more authentic part of me."[3]

My response to this continues to be, "Ugh. And AMEN."

The false self would have us believe just the opposite. The ego is always clamouring for attention: Look at me! To which the true self always says: *No way, pal. I am more than my flaws.*

When we practice wine, we pay attention. As we swirl, sniff, and sip in a tasting room or at a wine club, we learn about how it's grown, how it's made, and the people behind it. Through a singular focus on doing one thing with intentionality and purpose, we open to possibility. We cultivate curiosity and empathy, toward ourselves and others. We need more of that right now, don't we? So we can open to receive others—their stories, their lived experiences, their perspectives, their difference.

The Teigen-Boschman bond has been forged through years of sharing both joys and sorrows. Life is not meant to be a solo endeavour. We all need travelling companions, whatever leg of the journey we're on.

We need good pairings.

So, what if it's true? What if the practice of tasting wine can help you live out of your truest and best self?

> To stand in your truth.
> To find your voice.

To take the risk of being wrong.
To pay attention.
To get curious.

I've said a lot here about how wine tasting is a singular activity. I also see it as a **receptive** activity. There is a meditative dimension to tasting wine that can help us develop a posture of openness to God—a posture that, for many of us, is underdeveloped. In my training as a spiritual director, a useful awareness arose that my directees may not have done much work to cultivate a contemplative outlook in their lives. In other words, many people haven't given themselves to exercising openness in all the spaces we need to open: heart, mind, and body.

In their book, *The Practice of Spiritual Direction,* William Barry and William Connolly said:

> In the beginning phases of spiritual direction, directors usually have to help people to contemplate [or become open to] God. What kind of help do they need? They usually find that intensity and effort in looking at or listening to God are not very helpful; these usually end in self-absorption. They would benefit more from spending time at first in some activity they enjoy that has a contemplative aspect to it. [4]

Barry and Connolly go on to say that receptive experiences, like birdwatching, appreciating a city's architecture, listening to the surf (or to Bach), help directees to "forget themselves and become absorbed in something else." [5]

This list could absolutely include wine tasting.

Why not try this Wine Tasting as Spiritual Practice™ exercise?

The next time you have an opportunity to taste wine in an intentional, focused way, remind yourself that you're taking part in a receptive activity. Ask: How might this become an exercise in openness? As you begin tasting, focus on what happens in each of the three spaces mentioned above:

HEART

How does tasting this wine make you feel?
Can you name at least three emotions?

MIND

What does tasting this wine make you reflect on, wonder about, or imagine?

BODY

What happens in your body as you taste this wine?
Where exactly do you notice these sensations happening?
(Hint: your palate is probably one place.)

I'm not saying wine tasting is the only spiritual practice you'll ever need. Far from it. But I am saying it holds enormous potential to train us to open to God, to others, to ourselves, and to the world around us.

You know the feeling of being immersed in an activity you love. It's like you lose yourself. But if you stay in that place long enough or practice it often enough, something else happens: you begin to find yourself again. You realize you're part of something bigger, deeper, and wider than you can imagine. You wonder about that Mystery. You open to Love. You grow.

My WSET Level One taught me some basics about how different

foods impact the way your wine tastes. Ever brush your teeth and then drink orange juice right away? Big mistake, right? It tastes terrible—super acidic. And just weird. You make that face. The orange juice hasn't changed, of course. The toothpaste changed the way you experience the orange juice. The instructors made the point that the same thing happens when you taste wine immediately after ingesting food that's high in salt, acidity, sugar, fat, or spice. You perceive the wine as different.

We did several pairing experiments. Here's one you can try at home:

Grab a plate, and put a bit of salt, a lemon wedge, and a piece of old cheddar on it. (Old as in mature, not the spoiled stuff in the back of your fridge.)

Pour a glass of young Chianti Classico, or any red wine that has high acidity (makes your mouth water; usually on the sides of our tongues) and high tannin (causes that bitter, mouth-drying effect).[6]

Before tasting any food, have a sip of wine and concentrate on its astringency and bitterness.

Squeeze a few drops of lemon onto your tongue. Then add the salt and chew it.

Take another sip of wine. It'll be softer, fruitier, and smoother in texture.

Do the same with a bite of the salty cheddar and have another sip.

The fat in the cheese will make the wine seem even smoother and more velvety.

Our instructors referred to salt, acidity, and fat as the magic triangle.

These help soften up your palate before an acidic, tannic wine.

I'm only just beginning to learn about the principles and science behind wine pairings. And also the anecdotal secrets. Like when you pair wine with food, neither the food nor the wine should dominate or take over. They're meant to complement, to bring out the best in each other.

The pleasure and delight of wine are rarely just about the wine itself.

It's about the kind of food served alongside.
It's about the opportunities wine tasting affords—for personal growth, for human connection, for shared joy as well as sorrow, for the cultivation of empathy and receptivity.
It's about what goes with it.

And there's nothing like a great pairing.

CHAPTER EIGHT

The Shadow Side

It is not wise to become a drunk, for it will lead you to a life of emptiness and sorrow. Instead, drink deeply of Creator's Spirit, and he will lead you into a life of beauty and harmony.

—Ephesians 5:18, *First Nations Version*

In whatever you do, be moderate, and no addiction will afflict you... Wine is very life to humans, if taken in due measure. Does one really live who lacks the wine which was created from the first for his joy? Joy of heart, good cheer, and delight is wine enough, drunk at proper times. Headache, wormwood, and disgrace is wine drunk amid anger and strife.

—Jesus Ben Sira

One Monday evening, I told my spiritual direction group that I was about to head to a retreat centre to work on this book. They were all excited for me, one member especially so. She said, "Oh, that's great! My guys are gonna be up there! They're so sweet. You will absolutely love them."

Her guys were a group of men in a drug and alcohol recovery program from where she worked. I was like, "Ah, cool!"

I also felt a bit awkward.

A couple of days later, I boarded a ferry at dusk and sailed from Horseshoe Bay to Bowen Island. I drove up Cates Hill to Rivendell Retreat Centre, and sure enough, there were her guys. The next morning at eight o'clock, I joined some of them in a small circular sanctuary nestled in the woods. There, surrounded by lush forest and the sweet sound of birdsong, we spent twenty minutes together in centring prayer.

In the silence, whenever I got distracted, I came back to my sacred word: beloved. The symbol of my consent to whatever God wanted to do in me at that moment. At the same time, I became aware of the men I shared sacred space with, noticing that they too were deeply beloved.

It also struck me that their reasons for being at Rivendell couldn't have been more different than mine.

The guys were there to get as far away from alcohol as possible, to retreat from the substance(s) that had derailed their lives. They were there to find healing and freedom from addiction.

And I was there to write about the joy and blessing of an alcoholic beverage.

(Hence the awkwardness.)

I wrote most of this chapter on that same weekend. I never told the men exactly why I was there. I didn't feel guilty for writing about wine, not in the least. But I did feel compelled to think through how I would explain my book to a recovering alcoholic. I knew it would be important to acknowledge addiction and over-consumption at some point.

To name the shadow side.

Sidebar: I'll spend a bit more time in this chapter interacting intentionally with Scripture. That's because the arguments against consuming (any) alcohol are often religiously motivated. For a long time, certain verses, taken out of context, have fuelled assumptions that aren't necessarily based on the collective wisdom of biblical witnesses.

I said above that I am writing this book, as a Christian, with a totally clear conscience. I said that with gusto. Am I delusional? Given the prevalence of alcohol abuse around the world and its widespread and damaging effects, wouldn't we be better off to steer clear of it altogether?

Total abstinence is no new strategy. We saw it most clearly in the temperance movements of Great Britain and the United States.

In her excellent book, The Spirituality of Wine, Gisela Kreglinger summarizes the context well:

> The abuse of alcohol in the form of strong and cheap spirits such as gin and whiskey brought incredible suffering, especially to working-class people. Industrial workers would collect their meager earnings and take them straight to the pubs and bars, while their wives and children would go without

food and clothing. It is understandable that in such cases of widespread social evil, the only possible solution seemed to be to advocate complete abstinence.[1]

Kreglinger goes on to explain how, on the heels of the temperance movement, some interpreters argued that the Bible encourages complete abstinence. This view still exists today. It wasn't true then, and it isn't true now. Kreglinger quotes Martin Luther, priest, theologian, and a key figure of the Protestant Reformation.

Here's his provocative response to those who sought to forbid wine consumption in his day:

> Gold and silver, money and possessions bring much evil among the people, should we, therefore, throw it all away? If we want to eliminate our closest enemy, the one that is most harmful to us, we would have to kill ourselves. We have no more harmful enemy than our own heart.[2]

Luther understood that removing a potentially harmful thing does not solve the problem. Removal just shifts addictive habits to another part of our lives. In the same breath, Luther spoke strongly against the abuse of alcohol, as the German people in his time were pretty big fans of the Weingeist.[3] But rather than do away with it entirely, Luther called people of faith to be accountable for their actions. His experience taught him that the path to a whole and free life is to look within and examine our hearts: to see the underlying temptations, motivations, and misplaced affections that keep us moving in misguided directions. And to do this soul-level work in the presence of a compassionate, forgiving God.

If it's true that the scriptures do not teach total abstinence when it comes to alcohol, what do they have to say about overconsumption and misuse?

A deep dive into all the Bible has to say on these matters would take more time and space than we have here. Again, I refer you to Kreglinger and her thoroughly researched book for a broader treatment of this theme. Instead, I want to look at two contrasting images that I believe summarize Scripture's posture toward both the misuse and merits of alcohol.[4]

MISUSE AND ABUNDANCE

As you page through the Bible, you will never find a passage that portrays overconsumption as good. It's just not there. Alcohol misuse is always portrayed negatively. And wow, are there ever some doozies in there.

For example, the first person in the Bible to ever plant a vineyard was also the first person to ever get wasted out of his tree. Drunk Noah was not a pretty picture. He ended up in a state of utter undress, passed out au naturel in his tent. "A man of the soil," the scriptures called Noah. He was also, evidently, a man of the sauce.[5]

Then, there was the time Lot and his family narrowly escaped the destruction of Sodom of Gomorrah. As Lot and his two surviving daughters fled to the safety of a cave in the hills, there was an incident where too much wine plus incest led to Lot fathering children with them.[6]

The story of King David, Bathsheba, and her husband, Uriah, is another horrifying example of the shadow side of overconsumption. David seduces (read: rapes) Bathsheba, who becomes pregnant. David immediately summons Uriah from the field of battle to get him to come home and sleep with Bathsheba, thereby deflecting any "Who's the father?" suspicion. Uriah, being a stand-up guy, doesn't go home. He was like, "How could I go home and have sex with my wife when my troopmates are still out there fighting a war?"

So David comes up with Plan B: *I'll invite Uriah over for a bender. He'll drink himself silly. Surely inebriation will lead to procreation.*

Nope.
Uriah sleeps on a mat in the servants' quarters.

Foiled again, David stoops even lower and tells his army commander to put Uriah out front where the fighting was fiercest and then to withdraw so he'd be killed.

Plan C works. Third time's the charm.[7]

As alarming as these stories are, I'm glad they haven't been edited out of our Bibles. Why? Because, as in any good story, the warnings against misuse within Scripture do their work on us implicitly rather than explicitly. They do so through narrative.

I love the way author and spiritual teacher Brian McLaren talks about story:

> A story can't be argued with or dismissed like a proposition...a story is just sneaky. It doesn't teach by induction or deduction. It teaches by abduction. It abducts your attention and won't let you go until you have done some thinking for yourself.[8]

Stories like these sneakily cause us to think for ourselves about the plain fact that drunkenness usually ends poorly. That frequent over-indulgence almost always begets destructive, dehumanizing, violent behaviour. Still, in the face of such excess, grace abounds even more. God acts like a parent whose child is in trouble and hurting (both themselves and others). God comes close and says,

"I think you've learned your lesson."

There's a verse in the Psalms that says, *God gets angry once in a while, but across a lifetime there is only love.*[9]

As a father, a husband, and a human, I feel this deeply. There are certainly occasions when I get angry with my daughter, my wife, or myself. But we make it a practice to assure each other and our own souls: *No matter what, I will always love you.* (Cue Whitney Houston. And the tears.) We spell this out on fridge magnets, on Post-it notes, on t-shirts, wherever and whenever it's needed.

No matter what.

Was God upset by the foolish behaviour of Noah, Lot, and King David? Yes, without a doubt. Were their actions selfish and unjust? Absolutely. Even so, they didn't need further punishment for what they did. The natural consequences of their actions—the shame, the misuse, the violence—were punishment enough. (It's also important to recognize that the alcohol wasn't at fault in David's story. David was.)

And guess what? For all the stories that depict the dangers of drunkenness, Scripture speaks of wine as a blessing far more than it does as a curse.[10]

One symbol that shows up again and again—through the Old Testament prophets, for example—is wine as a gift from God. It gets even better. Where the misuse of wine leads to a wilful ignorance of God and others, the abundance of wine represents God's redemptive generosity toward God's people. As Kreglinger puts it, "God's people would forget to be a blessing to others, and would be unable to exercise justice and govern wisely."[11]

The prophet Isaiah put it this way:

Ah, you who rise early in the morning in pursuit of strong drink, who linger in the evening to be inflamed by wine, whose feasts consist of lyre and harp, tambourine and flute and wine, but who do not regard the deeds of the Lord, or see the work of his hands![12]

So, does the abundance of wine always point toward God's favour? Many argue that quantity is kind of the main problem. However, Scripture reveals that abundance becomes a sign of God's favour and generosity to the degree that it is *shared*.

This principle shows up in the stories, prayers, and prophet songs whether we're talking about wine, grain, or the land itself. Bounty swerves into misuse when it is stockpiled for oneself.

Imagine having a huge cellar filled with bottles you only drink alone. What a travesty.

In contrast, the person who receives wine with gratitude, as something to enjoy and share, sees it in truth:

A gift that displays Divine surplus.

Understanding wine as an image of abundance helps us centre God and others. Proper use always leads us deeper into community and connection.

Addictive misuse, however, keeps us solely focused on ourselves, which inevitably results in an inability to see what God is up to in the world. And we'd better have some real talk here. Aren't we all liable to compulsion and excess?

I'll let our pal Brené Brown answer that question. She said it about as well, and as plainly, as anyone:

> We all numb. We all have different numbing agents of choice—food, work, social media, shopping, television,

video games, porn, booze (from beer in a brown paper bag to the socially acceptable but equally dangerous "fine wine" hobby)—but we all do it. And when we chronically and compulsively turn to these numbing agents, it's addiction, not just taking the edge off. [13]

The moment we think we're immune to numbing is the moment we need to ask ourselves some hard questions.

Just what is addiction, anyway? I asked my friend Danny Taylor, an Addiction Prevention Specialist and Counselling Therapist, for a simple, clear definition. He said, "Addiction is a compulsive misuse of a substance, continuing regardless of the negative consequences, where one loses a sense of control over their drug use or activity (like technology, for example)." [14]

Danny went on to say that addiction is a complex issue. Many of us tend to assume it's a choice or a disease, but a much better (and more compassionate) understanding is to see addiction as a desperate attempt to solve the problem of pain. "Addiction is rarely an issue of the substance itself," he said. "It is always an issue of a person's very humanity." [15]

Brené speaks from experience on this. When she wrote those words, she had been sober for twenty years. She goes on to say, "There is no us and them when it comes to numbing—we all do it. The question is to what degree." [16]

So for the moment, let me gently but directly address those of us who fall into the category of fine wine hobbyists (or craft beer geeks, or whisky aficionados):

Who here's said, or felt, "Wow, that was a rough day. I sure could use a drink?"

That sentiment, which may begin as occasional, can easily become something frequent. What starts as an impulse once a month can become, before long, a weekly occurrence. "I could use a drink" becomes "I need a drink." That turns into a daily practice or habit. And if that's not kept in check, it can become an hourly impulse.

"I sure deserve a drink."
"I'm entitled to a drink."
"I can't live without a drink."

Although we may think we're not in danger of developing a full-blown alcohol addiction, each wine lover must take care to ensure our practice doesn't become uncontrollably compulsive.

Let me be extra-clear. This book's primary audience is not people in recovery. There are other books for that. I'm not an expert. If you or someone you know is struggling with addiction, I encourage you to seek help. I'm also not trying to be alarmist. But even as I seek to champion the benefits of moderate drinking—along with its accompanying enjoyments—we must also honour and hold the stories of those who struggle with addiction. We ignore the shadow side of wine at our peril.

No matter who you are, or where you are, or how much you drank last night, here are some self-check questions to carry with you:

Do I ever misuse wine (or any alcoholic beverage) as a numbing agent? When?

How might I recognize the signs that wine is becoming something more than enjoyable? Is becoming something dangerously compulsive?

What resources do I need to have on hand to make sure I use this gift (share it, enjoy it in moderation), not *misuse* it, as the Creator intended?

If I slip, where will I reach out? In my circle of relationships, who can I call upon to help me get back on a healthy track?

Let's return to Rivendell. To the small sanctuary in the trees.

On the surface, our reasons for being in that room, for being òn retreat, were seemingly opposite. Beneath the surface, however, something more like bedrock bound us together.

Each man in that room was beautiful, flawed, bruised-yet-whole. Made in the image of the Divine.
Not opposed to God.
Receiving redemption in real time.
Beloved.

Our reasons for going to Rivendell were different, but at the core, our motivation was the same. Each man in that room was there to engage life more fully and openly. To celebrate the extravagant, unfailing love in which Christ grounds our being. To be led deeper into community and connection—with God, with ourselves, with others.

Each man in that room was there to be filled with the Spirit, not emptied by drunkenness.

So now, dear reader, imagine yourself in that little sanctuary in the woods with those beloved men and with me. Sit as comfortably as you're able. Feel the ground beneath your feet. Take a moment to become still and quiet. When you're ready, receive this blessing:

May you learn to live free and full in a growing awareness of your Belovedness.
May you share your fill, sacrificially and generously, with those around you.
And may you be led by Creator's Spirit, ever more deeply and gently, into beauty, harmony, and abundance.

Yes.
Yes.
Yes

CHAPTER NINE

Taste and See

A beautiful mouthful of wine is a message from the soul:
Slow down enough to take things in. Life is quite absorbing
if you're not zipping through it.

—Terry Theise, *What Makes A Wine Worth Drinking*

Open your mouth and taste, open your eyes and see
how good God is.

—Psalm 34:8, *The Message*

Sometimes, I think it would be pretty awesome to be a sommelier.

More than tasting wine alone, one thing I love to do is introduce someone to a wine I've enjoyed in the past. Or to discover one together. Somms get to do that as a job. Wouldn't that be a great gig? Whenever I'm invited to a house party, I'm equally excited to celebrate the occasion as I am to pull the cork from a bottle and open myself to its delights.

Late one Friday night, I was at an engagement party for some dear friends. The couple had spent the earlier part of the evening together. Then, after (finally) getting engaged on a snow-capped mountain, they returned to the city where a houseful of friends and family lay in wait to surprise them.

It had all the makings of what people usually call a *fun night*. Good friends, good food and drink, good cheer, and bad jokes (the *I-hope-she-said-yes* as we waited for the couple to arrive). When they did show, the pair were liberally doused with love and celebration. I felt honoured to be there.

Why do I bring this up? Because, that night, I blundered big-time.

To set the scene, I first need to tell you that the Enneagram Nine vibes were off the charts for me that night.[1] Nines are often described as Adaptive Peacemakers. Here's what that looks like:

The need to feel settled, in harmony with everything.
The tendency to go along to get along.
The desire to avoid conflict at all costs.

Who wants peace at a party? Everyone.
Who wants conflict at a party? No one ever.
Who wants Nines at a party? Also everyone.

How did these vibes play out?

I had to decide which wine to bring. The invite had noted that a *small group of friends* would be present. Okay, so 15 to 20 people. I figured I'd pour some for a few friends, a glass for myself. I may even get a chance to share something about it with the *small group*.

What wine did I choose? A 2016 Le Vieux Pin Petit Rouge blend—mostly Merlot and Cabernet Franc, some Syrah. We're talking Old World, time-tested French winemaking, combined with the New World character of the Okanagan Valley. Remember Severine Pinte from Chapter 3? She made it. (Thanks for asking.)

I hadn't tasted this one yet, but was curious to try it and had been saving it for some time. It was not the most valuable bottle in my collection, but it was special and I knew it would be good. I never said any of this to anyone but myself. It was an engagement party, after all. And it was no real shocker to me that these people had zero interest in nerding out on wine.

Go along to get along.

Next, when I first arrived, a few bottles sat on the table in a large dining room. The house was packed, probably closer to 50 guests (not small), and no one had opened or consumed anything yet.

Carefully, I added my bottle to the others on the table.
I thought: *Yeah, the couple will be here soon, and then we'll crack stuff open. I'll just leave it here. It'll be fine.*

That's the Enneagram Nine fight song, by the way. *It'll be fine.*

And then, someone opened a bottle.

I was talking and laughing with a few friends when I noticed. I peeked into the dining room and sure enough. There was my bottle, disappearing fast. I was maybe ten feet away, but it felt rude to break off the conversation, you know, for wine. I couldn't find a good opening to get away and get some. Nines don't like conflict of *any* variety, but if we must choose between internal or external conflict, we'll almost always go with internal. So I'm standing there, flat-footed. Absorbing all these emotional body blows and no one else has a clue.

This was no time for good manners. I found an out and made my way toward the wine table. But a young thirtysomething dude snuck in there and beat me to it. He filled a massive glass with a generous portion, and that was that.

I glanced longingly at that precious, empty bottle. Then looked at the very full stemmed glasses people held firmly by the bowl. No swirl, no swish, and (at least in my mind) no proper savour. They just innocently drank some red wine at an engagement party.

I texted my friend the next morning:

There was inner conflict galore, but with me smiling and nodding and laughing the whole time. Because at the end of the day I brought the wrong bottle to this kind of party, so it was my own damn fault lol. #knowyouraudience

His response: *The layers! It ain't easy being Nine.*

Later, as I recalled the feelings from that night, I thought of a little exchange in Charlie Mackesy's delightful book, *The Boy, the Mole, the Fox and the Horse.* There's a hand-drawn illustration of a small boy sitting bareback on a white horse,[2] standing at the edge of a pond. A few feet away from them, two swans float peacefully on the surface of the water.

"How do they look so together and perfect?" asked the boy.
"There's a lot of frantic paddling going on beneath," said the horse.

Story of my life, I thought.

Lesson learned. Nerd-level wine tasting was clearly not the focus of that gathering.

That's the focus of Wine Club.

I'm incredibly grateful to have a group of like-minded, wine-loving friends I get to hang out with once a month to get geeky about wine. As you already know, Wine Club is one of my most life-giving, and therefore spiritual, practices. Let me say straight away that if you're reading this and going, *Wine Club, eh?* Must be nice, then I must tell you that it's not that hard to make one happen. To prove it, I'll give you a step-by-step process right here.

If you feel inspired and want to take the next steps to learn and grow in wine appreciation, here's one way:

Step One: Find a wine buddy

A partner in wine. One friend who shares a similar level of interest with you. Float the idea of getting together once a month or so to learn about and taste wine. If they latch onto the idea, you're in business. Like we all learned when we were kids, so long as there are two of you, you are officially a club.

Step Two: Find a few more buddies

It'll be richer, more fun, and more diverse. It'll also be easier to share the presenting and hosting tasks, as well as the budget.

Our group found that between seven and nine is ideal for ease of conversation, to cover all the duties, and to fit comfortably in an average-sized home in our city. Also, the standard wine bottle is 750ml, which means you have 25 ounces to share.

Our group is currently nine people. This means we taste just under three ounces of each wine, which is roughly half of a standard restaurant serving and a bit more than you'd get at a typical winery tasting. Definitely enough to savour, discover, compare, and enjoy. Pro tip: use a small measuring cup for portion accuracy.

Step Three: Set a rhythm and a structure

We decided that meeting monthly was right for us. Anything more would be unsustainable. Anything less, and we felt we might lose momentum. For us, a Wine Club night usually lasts about two and a half hours.

Between the nine of us, we take turns hosting and presenting.

The **host** provides a comfortable space. Somewhere you won't be interrupted. Ideally, there's a table where you can all sit down and see each other. The host also provides water glasses for everyone, plates for food, and charcuterie boards or anything else needed for serving.

If you want to get a bit fancy with candles, go for it. But no scented ones (!), since they will interfere with what you smell and taste in the wines.

The **presenter** purchases and brings four bottles on whatever theme they fancy (we share the cost. See Step Four). The presenter could focus on a specific wine region or sub-region. Or a specific grape variety. If you're in a warm season, it can be fun to compare patio wines, such as four different rosés.

One night, as the presenter, I chose "The Art of the Blend" as the theme, meaning all four wines were a blend of at least two varietals or types of grape. One had five or six varietals, and another had eleven. We had fun guessing which grapes were present in each wine.

Once the presenter decides on the theme, they research the wines: the region (or regions) they came from, the producers, the varietal (or varietals) used, any unique winemaking methods, stories, fun facts, etc. Because wine is such a big world to discover, whatever is of interest to the presenter is usually of interest to the group. And the options are endless.

When the night comes, the presenter shares what they've learned with the group. None of this, of course, has to be memorized or put into a fancy slide presentation. In our club, it's not uncommon for the presenter to bring their laptop along, have it open in front of them, and then share their notes afterward. The rest of us may take notes or simply listen. Often, the presenter will share for about ten or fifteen minutes before they pour the first wine. But you don't have to do it that way. You could share very little upfront and then slowly reveal your learnings as you taste the wines.

Speaking of learning, there are tons of resources out there. One that we've used every time is a printable tasting placemat.

Our crew uses the one from winefolly.com. It's standard letter size. Light cardstock is a nice touch if you have it, but normal white copy paper does the trick just fine. There are four circles on the mat, one for each wine glass. They're numbered, so you can keep track of which is which (especially if there's a blind tasting component on a given night).

Inside each circle is the heading Categories to Consider, beneath which is a list:

FRUIT
Berries, Citrus, Melon, Stone Fruit, Tree Fruit, Tropical

FLOWER
Dried, Fresh, Oils

SPICE
Possibly from Oak. Baking Spices, Sweet Spices, Exotic Spices

HERB
Dried, Fresh

EARTH
Mineral, Dirt, Texture (from Tannin)

OTHER
Smoke, Wood-like Aromas, Petroleum, Rubber, Tar

Popped out from each circle are a few blank lines where you can write down the Region/Country where the wine is from and other details such as producer name, varietal/s, and vintage (harvest year).

Beneath those deets are two horizontal lines. One is for marking the Fruit Level you detect in the wine, on a scale from *fruity* to *earthy*. The other is for Body, somewhere between *light* and *bold*. (A widely used analogy to assess body is to consider how skim milk, whole milk, and cream feel in your mouth. That's a helpful scale to determine whether a wine is light, medium, or full-bodied.)

Back inside the circle, at the bottom of each, is a human face with two eyes but no mouth. That's where you can note your overall impression of the wine.

A smile means "yay." *I can't wait to drink this again.*

A straight line means "meh." *Sure, I could drink this again, but I'm not gonna go out of my way to hunt it down.*

A frown means "boo." *I'd be content if I never had to drink this again as long as I live. But it was a good learning experience (as every wine tasting is).*

These placemats are a great way to focus your learning. They help you direct and organize your thoughts about each wine you taste in a non-pretentious way. There are super-detailed ones available. But for anyone not engaged in industry-level training, the free, downloadable PDF versions are all that's needed.[3]

Some of us have purchased another useful tool: an aroma wheel, or Wine Flavour Finder. They are designed to help develop our palates by identifying flavours in wine and from where they emerge.[4] They do this by expanding the categories listed above. For example, on a flavour wheel under the heading of FRUIT, there are several colour-coded spokes in the wheel. One is for red fruit, specifically: cranberry, red plum, pomegranate, sour cherry, plus four or five others. Another is for tropical fruit: pineapple, mango, guava, and more. There's a spoke for FLOWER: iris, peony, jasmine, honeysuckle. And one for SPICE: white pepper, cinnamon, mint, and thyme.

You get the idea. A cool gift for the wine nerd in your family (which, let's face it, is probably you).

Step Four: Set a budget

This varies according to what people in your club can afford (or feel they can invest), and how seriously they want to explore different wine regions, varietals, or producers. For example, you can easily do an evening focused on Cabernet Sauvignon for a budget like the one I'm about to outline for you. But if you want there to be a higher quality Cab from Napa Valley in the mix, be prepared to either: go over budget, take significant cost-cutting measures when selecting your other three, or set up a side fund.

We decided on $20 (Canadian currency) per person, per night. For a group of nine, this yields a total budget of $180. Of that amount, we spend $160 each time we meet. Usually, that breaks down into about $120 for wine and $40 for snacks. Then we put the remaining $20 in a side fund for times when we may want to splurge a bit more. For example, one time I co-presented on sparkling wines with another club pal. She and I wanted to have the group try at least one bottle of actual Champagne, which tends to cost significantly more than other types of bubbly.[5] Thanks to the side fund, we were able to do that.

Step Five: Schedule your first three nights

You could simply book the first one and go from there. But we found it helpful to lock down at least a few dates. We've often got busy schedules and it's wise to commit. Having three Wine Club dates in your calendar also helps build anticipation.

All this fun, of course, can only remain fun if everyone gets home safely. We always stay within the amounts we've set and serve the portions equally. No opening extra bottles unless designated drivers or public transit are available, or folks can get home on foot. Moderate consumption, plus snacks and water over time, ensures that Wine Club stays safe.

Now that you know what one example of a wine club looks like, let me come back to the initial thought of this chapter: I love introducing people to good wine. This is probably my favourite aspect of presenting at Wine Club. I'm not a sommelier, but, not gonna lie, there are times I dream about becoming one. And on Wine Club nights where I'm the presenter, I get to pretend I am.

I rarely dine at restaurants that have somms. When I do, I get a little giddy. It was mid-July. My wife Terri and I were out on a date. We went to a place called *The Wine Bar,* which was about a five-minute walk from where we lived at the time. It's one of the places to go in Vancouver if you want wine variety with excellence. They have over 200 wines available by the glass, including nearly fifty on tap.

You can create your own custom tasting flights. You can even set your own portion size (within reason). That night, I told the sommelier I wanted to do a flight of three French wines—just two ounces each, so as not to break the bank.

"That sounds great," he said. "What are some of your favourites? What do you like to drink?"
"I like a pretty wide range," I replied. "Which is the main reason I love coming here! If I had to choose one region to drink from for the rest of my life, and if money were no object, it would probably be Burgundy."

Money was an object, however, and the best Burgundies ain't cheap. So I looked elsewhere.

"Ok, I'll let you peruse. Let me know if you have any questions."

I had never tried red wines from Provence, so I chose two from the sub-region of Bandol, made mostly from Mourvèdre, the main grape in the area, with a touch of Grenache.

The first was a delightful blend by Domaines Bunan: the 2014 Moulin des Costes Bandol Rouge. Blackberry, blueberry, cedar, oak, vanilla, and a bit of astringency that probably would have been better with lamb, had I ordered some. But still very good.

The second was another 2014 Bandol Rouge, this one from producer Bastide de la Ciselette. Blackberry and plum, with hints of tobacco and leather. A beautiful, pleasing balance of fruit and earth.

The third was also from France, but beyond that, I *didn't* know. I had asked the sommelier to surprise me. Because I'm always up for a mini blind tasting.

I admired its colour: a medium-dark ruby/garnet hue. I swirled and sniffed. *Hmm, what is this? Dark-ish in colour, but I'm picking up more red fruit than black. Cherry, raspberry...what else? Strawberry, a bit of earth.*

I looked, swirled, and sniffed again. In all honesty, I probably did that about five or six times before taking a sip. And then eventually, I did. *Gosh, this is delicious.* It was not exactly like anything I'd had before. But it bore similarities to other wines I'd tasted.

The somm came by. "So? What do you think?"
"I love it! And I'm so curious to know what it is!" I said. I decided to hazard a guess. "Is this Pinot? It's not Burgundy, is it?"
"Not exactly, no. But you're not far off."

It was Beaujolais.

Beaujolais (bow-zhuh-LAY), which is rather fun to say, has long been considered part of Burgundy, but has carved out its own lane in the wine landscape.

I was surprised and delighted.

Surprised because it wasn't how I assumed Beaujolais would taste. I'd assumed Bojo was always light in colour, with mostly red fruit flavours, and without much depth or complexity, let alone any earthiness to balance it out. (My assumption isn't entirely unfounded. Google "Beaujolais Nouveau" if you're curious. Obviously, I was mistaken.)

I was delighted to discover great value in a new French region. The wine was the 2017 Domaine Mathieu & Camille Lapierre from Morgon. Morgon is one of the ten *crus* of Beaujolais. Cru translates as "growth," but more accurately refers to a broadly-recognized-as-superior growing site or vineyard. At my local wine shop, a bottle of Morgon made by Mathieu & Camille Lapierre costs about $47. But it drinks like a wine worth nearly twice that amount.

Later that night, I wrote my review on Vivino, a popular wine app I use to track wines I've tried, read community-based reviews, and create wish lists. It began with the words, *I need to drink more Beaujolais.*

Early September. I'm back at the same spot with some buddies for a birthday hangout. It was a warm evening. I started with a BC Chardonnay. Then I found that same Morgon on the menu. This time, I upgraded from two ounces to a whole fiver.

That Beaujolais, enjoyed with good pals, was a highlight of my night. Partly because someone else paid for it.

As I swirled those black cherry, strawberry, leathery aromas up into my nose, I thought: *Wine Club needs to drink more Beaujolais.*

Et voilà: the next time I was on to present, you gotta know it was Bojo Night.

Have you ever been hosted by a good sommelier?

And I don't mean "good" in the sense that they know their stuff and can upsell even the most frugal guest. I mean good in the sense that they make a connection. Good in the sense that they offer you a curated taste experience you'll remember.

Master Sommelier Dustin Wilson of Verve Wine notes an evolution in how wine drinkers see somms: "The perception of what a sommelier was 20 to 30 years ago was this snooty old guy who wanted to talk down to you and try to get you to buy the most expensive thing... The best way to beat that stigma is to go completely in the opposite direction and say, 'we're here to make wine super fun, really approachable.'" [6]

I think he's right. The best somms help make wine enjoyable and accessible. Which isn't to say they'll always default to what they know you'll like. A good somm can also sense when you might be ready to try something new. And they'll work to discover the degree of newness you're open to, as mine did.

He knew I was serious about wine. He knew I was curious to try new things. And he knew I liked Burgundy.

I picked two from a region that was new to me, and then asked him to surprise me with the third. He chose a wine that would feel like familiar territory, but would also open me up to an entirely new region and simultaneously broaden my palate.

That's when things get exciting. You learn that a wine can surprise you. Your palate develops and expands. You discover great value. You become more attuned to your body as you engage senses with the sights, smells, and tastes of lovingly crafted food and drink.

I've come to think of the psalmists as the sommeliers of Scripture.

The psalmeliers, if you will.

Psalmeliers are forever calling our attention to physical senses and metaphor as ways to experience God.

Right off the bat, in Psalm 1, a person who delights in God's teaching is likened to a fruit-bearing tree.[7]

Turn a few pages to Psalm 8, where we might imagine the psalmist lying on her back, gazing in awe at a star-filled night sky, wondering aloud at God's attention toward her, toward each of us.[8]

In Psalm 18, the psalmelier points us toward several images through which to perceive the Divine and offer our prayers:

> *I love you, God—*
> *you make me strong.*
> *God is bedrock under my feet,*
> *the castle in which I live,*
> *my rescuing knight.*
> *My God—the high crag*
> *where I run for dear life,*
> *hiding behind the boulders,*
> *safe in the granite hideout.[9]*

And on it goes.

Here's one more:

Taste and see that the Lord is good.[10]

It's a fascinating phrase. The psalmelier calls us to engage our senses to appreciate the Unseen Divine. This is an invitation into the abstract and out of the literal. We can't taste or *see* God. It's nothing short of an invitation to impossibility. And yet there it is, in the middle of the ancient prayer book known as the Psalms, without apology or explanation.

I've always been curious as to why it doesn't say, "Hear and understand that the Lord is good." After all, these verbs are commonly connected and regarded as ways we interact with God.

I have to believe the reasons were more than poetic.

What if a vibrant spirituality is meant to be more than cognitive understanding? What if faith is not primarily mental assent to a list of beliefs, but a way of being? How is it that so much religious life has treated humans not as multisensory beings, but as a mere brain on a stick?

These are huge questions, and we don't have the time or space to engage them all. I want to invite you to ask them through the lens of your own experience. To humbly consider whether there might be more to your life with God than what you've assumed.

Like good wine, life in and with God is meant to be savoured, enjoyed, embodied, experienced as good.

After times of fun and feasting, you need downtime. After producing a rich harvest, a vineyard needs to rest. That's where we're going next. Before we turn the page, though, I invite you to revel in goodness. A few questions to sit with as you do:

What might it look like to "taste and see" a little more than you do now?

Who are the soul somms in your life? The people who help you notice where and how God might be present and active in the growing seasons of your life? How could you offer that same attentiveness to someone else struggling to experience Divine Presence in their life?

Who will you call on to be your first official wine buddy?

CHAPTER TEN

Winter Among the Vines

I'm beginning to understand a bit more, now in my middle-aged years, that trust in God grows best when things are falling apart; or as the seventeenth-century Scottish theologian Samuel Rutherford said, "Grace grows best in winter."
—Pete Enns, *The Sin of Certainty*

As the year turns, the wine-making families go out in ones and twos, to prune their vines. This will make the rootstalk stronger for the next harvest. They burn the deadwood right here in the field. The ashes fall to the ground, making good natural fertilizer. This is something they've done for hundreds of years. But then, there's a lot of things they do in Burgundy they've been doing for hundreds of years. In a couple of months—exactly when, who knows—the first signs of spring will come again. And then, it'll be another year in Burgundy.
—David Kennard (writer), *A Year in Burgundy*

I never thought I'd be a college professor.

It's not one of those jobs you talk about with your pals in grade three, you know? I mean, back then, we hardly knew what college was. Firefighter. NBA star. Dentist. That's what made the list. College prof? Not so much.

Years pass. Seasons change. You grow a little. Eventually, you realize you need a new list. One that has to do with an inner sense of calling and not just a paycheque.

I never thought I'd be a college professor.
Then, all of a sudden, I became one.

At 27, I joined the Worship Arts faculty at Columbia Bible College in Abbotsford, BC. I taught students how to do music at church. (As well as worship through other art forms, as our program title, "Worship Arts," suggests). Twenty-seven is pretty young. At least it felt that way to me. Which is why inwardly I went *Yesss!* whenever I came across videos that were usable as course content. Because what student alive in the 90s *didn't* like it when their young, hip professor rolled the ol' TV/VHS cart into the classroom?

In 1996, Randy and Terry Butler produced a video called *Worship Team Dynamics.* The Butlers were musical worship leaders within the Vineyard denomination. I don't know how many times I watched and used and shared that video during my early years teaching and leading workshops. And I know it made the rounds beyond my classroom. I searched for it online, and sure enough, someone uploaded it to YouTube, with Spanish subtitles. *Worship Team Dynamics* lives![1]

At the time, I was almost as excited about that video as I was when I first heard *Did You Feel The Mountains Tremble?* by Delirious. If you were part of a church that had a worship band, *Worship*

Team Dynamics fell in the category of essential viewing. Why? Because the Butler duo touched on several key principles and demonstrated them with their instruments and voices.

They talked about arranging. About the need for simplicity. And how just because you're in the band, doesn't mean you need to be busily strumming or plunking away on your instrument *all* the time.

Before joining Columbia's teaching faculty, I also worked there for three years as an Admissions Counsellor—a role that took me to many different churches. I'd seen some terrible worship bands. As far as I was concerned, the church needed to pick up what the Butlers were putting down.

At one point in the film, Randy said, "It's gotta get quiet sometimes."

In context, he was speaking of quiet in the sense of: music still happening, but not quite as loud. I understood what he was saying. And as a musician, I agree. But I also heard this as a more fundamental, all-encompassing call for quiet, period. The need to not have music—or other noise, or audible stimulus—happening all. the. time.

The need for spaciousness.
Sparseness.
A pause.

The need for
silence.

Silence in worship, certainly. But also in life.
In our homes.
In our workplaces.
In nature.

It's gotta get quiet sometimes.

I tucked that away. I encouraged my students to consider how to create spaces for quiet in the way they led others. I took baby steps in my journey around the intentional practice of silence.

And what better way to do that than to hang out with monks?

There's a tiny village in the Burgundy region of France called Taizé (tay-ZAY). Taizé is home to a monastic community that welcomes thousands of visitors each year. In August of 2006, my colleague, Tony Funk, and I made a pilgrimage to spend a week with the Taizé Community. (I embarrassingly admit that, at the time, I knew nothing about the significance of this region to the wine world.)

The Taizé Community started in 1940 by Roger Schütz, or Brother Roger, at age twenty-five (and here I thought twenty-seven was young). Brother Roger left his native home of Switzerland and immediately set out to help people living under the horrors of World War II—something his grandmother did during the First World War. He settled in the small village of Taizé, which, due to its proximity to the demarcation line that divided France in two, was well-placed to shelter refugees fleeing the war. Friends from Lyon began giving the address of Taizé to those in search of safety.

More than just physical shelter, Brother Roger's vision for Taizé was to create a community. When asked why, he said, "When I was young, I was astonished to see Christians talking about God of love while at the same time wasting so much energy in justifying oppositions. And I said to myself: to communicate Christ, is there anything more transparent than a life that is given, a life where day after day reconciliation is accomplished concretely?"[2]

Brother Roger deliberately invited both Protestant and Catholic brothers to join him in forming an ecumenical monastic community. One that would intentionally work to build bridges of peace and reconciliation between people groups who may well believe different things about God, but who felt that what united them was greater than what divided them.

What's happening at Taizé is radical and unprecedented. And I got to see it for myself.

Tony and I were there with six thousand others.
Yes, you read that right. Not sixty, or six hundred. Six thousand. Mostly between the ages of 16 and 25. Each took a week of their summer to hang out with monks who had made a lifelong commitment to following Christ in simplicity, celibacy, and community.

Taizé ain't no ordinary summer camp.
It was a decidedly non-North American experience.

One that's been going on for years. Tony referred to it as Europe's longest-running revival movement.

(By the way, I was 35 at the time, and my colleague was 45. We were among the two or three hundred old-timers. Which made us feel not *totally* like fish out of water, but close.)

We gathered with the brothers for worship three times daily: morning, early afternoon, and evening. We sat on the floor in a room filled with candles and icons. We sang short, repetitive chants in about a dozen different languages. We listened to the scriptures read aloud. And we sat in silence. For anywhere from four to eight minutes at a time. With six thousand other people.

Here's how the Taizé Community describes their schedule:

Three times a day, everything on the hill of Taizé stops: the work, the Bible studies, the discussions. The bells call everyone to church for prayer. Hundreds or even thousands of mainly young people from all over the world pray and sing together with the brothers of the community. Scripture is read in several languages. In the middle of each common prayer, there is a long period of silence, a unique moment for meeting with God.[3]

I knew enough about Taizé before I arrived to know that silence would be a regular part of the experience. Even though I'd begun to value silence, I still had apprehensions about being in it with any regularity for longer than just a few seconds. And with other people.

Can you imagine what it would be like to hold eight minutes of silence with six thousand other members of the human family? Every soul in the room, being still before the Divine Presence. Holding space for others in prayer. Not trying to control, fix, manipulate, or bend the hand of God to our finite human wills. Six thousand souls seeking a better way, holding silence to practice alignment with God's will:

Your kingdom come, your will be done on earth, as Jesus taught us to pray.

Well.

By my second day there, I looked forward to the silence the most. It was incredible. A place that revered and practised silence helped me become aware of my own need for it.

I love how the Taizé Community speaks of silent prayer:

If we take as our guide the oldest prayer book, the biblical Psalms, we note two main forms of prayer. One is a lament and cry for help. The other is thanksgiving and praise to God. On a more hidden level, there is a third kind of prayer, without demands or explicit expression of praise. In Psalm 131 for instance, there is nothing but quietness and confidence: "I have calmed and quieted my soul... hope in the Lord from this time on and forevermore."

At times prayer becomes silent. Peaceful communion with God can do without words. "I have calmed and quieted my soul, like a weaned child with its mother." Like the satisfied child who has stopped crying and is in its mother's arms, so can "my soul be with me" in the presence of God. Prayer then needs no words, maybe not even thoughts.[4]

It's gotta get quiet sometimes.

So we can hear.
So we can remember.
So we can grow our capacity to love across difference.

"A moment of silence, even very short, is like a holy stop, a sabbatical rest, a truce of worries."[5] In our busy, bustling, excessively verbal existences, what else can we do without words?

During that week at Taizé, I started to become friends with silence. It's a friendship that has only grown and deepened over time. Sometimes in fits and starts, because noise tends to be relentless. But I can honestly say, silence and I are on better terms today than ever before.
It has to get quiet sometimes.

It's a matter of life and death.

Just ask the earth.

Wine columnist Matt Kramer said that one of the most important trends in wine these days is a growing awareness about dirt: "The complexity of it. The life diversity within it. And somehow, wine's ability to reflect the living world of dirt."[6]

The wine world is talking dirt. "In a word," says Kramer, "soil is alive. Or should be. The famous soils scientist Hans Jenny of the University of California Berkeley once estimated that if you total up all the microbial, invertebrate, and vertebrate life underground, one acre contains the biomass equivalent of ten draft horses."[7]

The problem? The dirt is dying. In recent decades, the earth beneath our vineyards has been in agony due to over-cultivation. Some believe that if this pattern continues, our best wines will suffer.[8]

My Inner Cynic, sitting on my shoulder, reads that sentence and says:

That's an awfully privileged perspective for more sustainable environmental practices. Poor baby. The earth is dying, and your wine's gonna get a little less tasty. Don't we have bigger fish to fry?

But then this other voice, perched on my other shoulder (That Inner Voice Who Truly Does Care?), pipes up:

No, pay attention. Give the soil a break now and then and, not only will the soil benefit, but the entire ecosystem will. All of it. The whole shebang.

Life is leaching from Europe's soils. Possibly due to centuries of cultivation. So, European winegrowers are taking the lead to address this issue. Now, for the first time, there are more traditional vineyards growing a single crop. Never before has the land been so monocultural. The "unbroken carpet of vines" that span from the Côte-d'Or in France to Barbaresco in Italy didn't exist until the 1960s. Prior to that, the land was a hodgepodge of vineyard and pasture.[9]

What's happening in many intensely cultivated vineyards—to say nothing of other types of farmland—is a disturbingly rapid process called *soil life exhaustion* (aka soil fatigue, soil erosion, or soil degradation). Soil fatigue is most often caused by the toxic trio of: chemical entrants into soils, farming with heavy machinery, and the extensive loss of trees, whose root systems are crucial to soil health.[10]

The leading researchers on soil fatigue are Claude and Lydia Bourguignon. The Bourguignons are agronomists who, since 1989, have surveyed and studied over 12,000 soils all over the wine world.[11] Their findings are alarming. In France, for example, soils have decreased from containing 2000kg of earthworms per hectare in the 1950s to less than 100kg today. What many people don't realize is that the soil's fauna, like worms and other insects, are essential in producing organic matter that vineyards need to grow.[12]

Fortunately, a growing number of top winemakers are paying attention to the Bourguignons' research, joining their cause to ensure that these precious soils are recalled to life. The work of soil-reinvigoration is multi-faceted, of course. A big part of it involves preparing natural infusions that attract earthworms, who then burrow deep into the dirt and expand drainage potential. They also huddle around decaying matter to churn out vermi-compost, "a kind of supercharged soil rejuvenator."[13]

It may be too early to tell if you can taste the difference these efforts make in their wines. But the producers consulting with the Bourguignons can at least assure the rest of us that their soils are now more full of life. Which alone is worth the effort.

You can't work the soil continually, without stopping, without rest.

It's gotta get quiet sometimes.

The same is true in the soil of our lives.

Consider the lilies, Jesus said.[14]

Saunter through the vineyards. Recognize your connection to all of life. You and I cannot keep plodding along forever without pause, without ceasing. Always talking and never holding our tongues.

At the same time, we must recognize that silence and stillness aren't the only requirements. The wise teacher said:

> *There's a time for everything and a season for everything*
> *under the heavens:*
> *a time to be born and a time to die,*
> *a time to be silent and a time to speak,*
> *a time to love and a time to hate,*
> *a time for war and a time for peace.*[15]

Winter in the vineyard, a fallow season of silence, reminds us of our need for seasons. Of spring and of ceasing. Still, the vineyard can surprise. Weather conditions and unexpected, disruptive circumstances can remind us that good care calls us to stillness and rest, and also to diligent, intentional action.

At the end of my sabbatical in 2018, my family and I got to visit Bordeaux, France. We spent most of our month-long stay near the Saint-Émilion appellation (or sub-region). Since then, I started following a few producers from that area on social media. One night as I was scrolling through my Instagram feed, I came across a striking video. It showed footage of a vineyard in Saint-Émilion at night. Frost was on the ground, and hundreds of small fire pots lined the rows.

The caption read, "A year ago, we won the fight against frost with fire." The date of the post? April 18, 2020.[16]

Frost isn't always bad for vineyards. It all depends on the time of year. It can actually be a very good thing in winter. A few weeks of heavy frost in December, January, or February often helps reduce the population of ticks and other unwanted bugs or fungi. The problem is when frost occurs in late March or April when there has been a warm spell in early March. Once the vine has started its growth cycle, all those tiny buds are exposed.

Late frost descended upon Saint-Émilion that year. In those moments, winegrowers tap into their deepest reservoirs of creativity to cope with the unexpected.

While we must be vigilant about taking seasons of sleep, rest, and dormancy, there is also the need to guard against inactivity becoming one's default pattern.

A time for everything...

We need silence, yes, but there's also a time to speak. To stand against injustice. To look out for December conditions in April. To face the unpredictable events and fight against that which threatens new birth with death.

How do you cultivate preparedness for action?
What if silence and rest are a huge part of that preparation?

Father Richard Rohr named his organization the *Center for Contemplation and Action* out of a firm belief that these two ways of being must be linked together. And that instruction in the contemplative way ought to take priority.

In what I think is one of his best books, *Everything Belongs* (if you haven't read it yet, you should immediately get a hold of a copy and read it. Next, I mean—after you finish mine.), he writes:

> This may seem odd, coming from a Center...that works to improve people's lives and is committed to social change, but...I'm convinced that I must primarily teach contemplation. I've seen far too many activists who are not the answer. Their head answer is largely correct but the energy, the style, and the soul are not. So if they bring about the so-called revolution they are working for, I don't want to be part of it (especially if they're in charge). They might have the answer, but they are not themselves the answer. In fact, they are often part of the problem.[17]

Rohr goes on to say that this form of noisy, reactive activism is why so many revolutions ultimately never achieve their end goal: "they self-destruct from within." [18] Instead, he suggests, we ought to follow the example of Jesus and other great spiritual teachers into a steady, ongoing change of our inner posture. Instead of floating down the current of an ego-driven culture, Rohr encourages the contemplative pathway, which will inevitably bring us face to face with our go-to patterns of control, addiction, tension, anger, and fear.

"When Jesus is led by the Spirit into the wilderness," Rohr writes, "the first things that show up are wild beasts (Mark 1:13). Contemplation is not first of all consoling. It's only real." [19]

I can sure attest to that. My growth cycle in the contemplative journey got kick-started over two decades ago. Taizé was a big part of it, as were the worship video people.

It has not always been easy. But the more I dig deeper into the soil of my Made-In-The-Image-of-God self—paying attention, listening, and learning—the more I am rejuvenated by Love. I am sustained and nourished by the practices of silence and attentiveness to my inner landscape. Which is where we all first and foremost encounter the Divine.

The contemplative way can be hard work. No question about it. And the action it inevitably leads us to take part in also requires energy, capacity, and effort. But I've recently discovered a new angle on silence and rest that has set my body, mind, and spirit abuzz. An angle that brings contemplation and action together in a single practice. It's a way to re-frame rest so that contemplation is the action.

The Nap Ministry is a movement founded by Tricia Hersey (she's the "bishop" of the movement and one of my new heroes) in 2016. Hersey is a performance artist, theatremaker, activist, theologian, and community healer. The Instagram profile of The Nap Ministry reads: "We examine the liberating power of naps. We believe rest is a form of resistance and reparations." [20]

Curious to hear more? Same here. To give you more of an idea of what this beautiful and inspiring and important movement is all about, here are a few quotes (Full disclosure: It was all I could do to stop from including more).

Fortify your hearts with rest. Rest is part of our resistance.

A Black Woman in a rested state is a radical act.

We don't want a seat at the table. F#*k the table. The table is full of oppressors. We want a blanket and a pillow down by the ocean. We want to rest.

We are bound up in so many ways because we have accepted exhaustion as normal.

Many people see grind culture as this pie-in-the-sky monster when it's actually your individual behaviours daily, constantly requesting more and more from people and living in a state of urgency about non-urgent things. Deep healing around your trauma is necessary. Decolonize.

You are not a machine. Stop grinding.

My body is an antenna for infinite ideas and inventions when I rest, nap, sleep and daydream.

Our lives are a beautiful experiment in curiosity and creation. We can craft a life outside of the toxic systems. Why collective care, imagination and rest is so vital to our liberation. Without them, we will not make it.

See what I mean?

I feel like screaming this stuff from the top of buildings. I kinda think that'd be worthwhile.

For some reason, we've allowed a narrative to take root that inactivity, quiet, and rest equal unaccomplishment. Tricia Hersey and other Black theologians and activists, who are rooted in a contemplative tradition, are right: it's gotta stop. We need to decolonize and detox ruthlessly.

In a worship gathering, silence is not 'dead air.'

If it's hard to imagine what this might look like, let me lay a few more pearls of wisdom on you from The Nap Ministry.

Here are three guiding principles for Rest Practice.

> 1. *Do not argue or debate with strangers online. This is valuable daydreaming and "resting my eyes" time. Social media and technology are leading us to the path of exhaustion. Detox regularly.*
>
> 2. *You can say NO more to make space for rest time. What's for you will come to you. You don't have to be thirsty for everything offered. Your calendar is a sacred text.*
>
> 3. *Work on your ego. Participate in shadow work and healing trauma. Realize that a lot of your workaholic ways are because of your ego. Examine this. You don't have to do everything.*

In the vineyard, so in life.

To let the soil rest for a time means the vines will keep producing for the long haul.

What might your practice of silence bring forth?

What fruit can grow in your life when you make the often-difficult, counter-cultural choice to keep quiet, lie down, and rest?

A good friend often reminds me that a poem often says things better than prose. So, as winter among the vines draws to a close, I leave you with a poem.

Keeping Quiet
If we were not so single-minded
about keeping our lives moving,
and for once could do nothing,
perhaps a huge silence
might interrupt this sadness
of never understanding ourselves
and of threatening ourselves with death.
Perhaps the earth can teach us
as when everything seems to be dead in winter
and later proves to be alive.
—Pablo Neruda

SOIL

CHAPTER ELEVEN

Somewhereness, Revisited

Those of us who credit the existence of terroir, of its legitimacy as a metaphor for understanding the natural world, know that recognizing terroir is no more—and no less—than a way of being alert.

—Matt Kramer

O Master, let me not seek as much to be consoled as to console, to be understood as to understand, to be loved as to love...

—St. Francis of Assisi

If you enjoy wine for reasons beyond its capacity to intoxicate, I wonder if, once upon a time, someone introduced you to it like people introduce you to a good friend: "Oh, you have GOT to meet her!"

Or like my friend Disc Golf Paul (from the Introduction), who stood at the edge of a disc golf course and wildly waved me in. If you're a fan of wine, it could be that your cork popped differently.

Shared enthusiasm did it for me. It was caught, not taught.

The relationship with wine I have today didn't happen overnight. It wasn't love at first sip. My appreciation has deepened over time. And it took more than one enthused human to get me to that place. I remember the times when I noticed a shift. Moments when wine and I took our relationship to the next level.

It was a comfortably warm summer evening. The sort that begs a patio, conversation, and culinary delights. My pal Lance wanted to introduce me to a friend visiting from out of the country who also shared a passion for wine. This friend, I'll call David, also happened to be "a man of means" and a generous one at that.

We made our way to the patio at, you guessed it, *The Wine Bar*. A slight breeze blew off the water as we settled in. We had a lovely view of the seawall, which was full of people walking strollers and dogs—laughing, chatting, and licking gelato in waffle cones. After we each had a glass of whatever we fancied, along with some crispy calamari with piquillo pepper aioli and lemon, David suggested we share a bottle. He was covering the bill, so I knew we'd get to punch above our weight class that night.

It was no use trying to hide my guileless excitement. My heart started picking up tempo as I reached for the gloriously long, beautifully curated list of available bottles. I let my eyes veer down to the typically off-limits part of the wine list. I was woefully unable to turn my ear-to-ear grin into a chill and completely normal mouth shape.

Being the gracious, generous host he was, David asked what we'd discovered lately and what we were curious to try.

Lance knew this meant more to me than it would to him. He wanted me to narrow the search, so he waited for me to respond. A characteristically gracious and selfless gesture. I waited, too, for about three seconds. (Don't wanna appear rude, ya know?) Then I spoke up.

"Well, red Burgundy is the holy grail for me right now. I've only had it a couple of times, but it has opened a whole new depth of complexity, aromas, and flavours that I'd never encountered before."

As we all know by now, Burgundy is one of France's most well-known wine regions. Many would argue that Burgundy continues to produce the world's finest wine from the Pinot Noir varietal.

David said, "Yeah, I hear that. I'm a fan as well. Have you ever had Burgundy that's a little older?" (I hadn't.) And then, "Let's see if we can find something with a bit of age on it."

Sure enough, there was a 2003 Louis Jadot Gevrey-Chambertin Champeaux on the list. We were about to enjoy a Premier Cru Burgundy. A fifteen-year-old Premier Cru Burgundy. [1]

The somm poured the wine, and we clinked our glasses in hushed reverence toward one another, the moment, and this incredible liquid. Then I looked, swirled, sniffed, and sipped.

I don't recall exactly what I said, but I remember the feeling. It was like, *Goodness me. There is a lot going on here.* If you could hear my wine love expanding like you can hear bamboo grow, you'd hear an audible *click, click, click* through the rest of that unforgettable evening.

In many ways, every chapter I've written here is a growth chart measuring the slow, steady increase of my enthusiasm for wine. I've tried to share every story I can remember. A well-curated tasting experience, a vineyard tour, a conversation with a fellow enthusiast, a night on a patio sipping Burgundy. I can look back. I can trace the slow but steady growth of my roots, of my wine endearment, as they crawl deeper into the soil of my life.

It takes time to develop a true appreciation for anything or anyone. The kind that goes beyond what that thing or person can do for you. The kind of appreciation that is too good to keep to yourself.

Think about these words from wine critic James Suckling: "I want you to look forward to every glass, but at the same time, I want you to understand what's in that glass, what went behind it, who made it, where it came from, and why it's so good."

I don't know every reason why Mr. Suckling wants you and me to understand all these things about wine. Given that this quote appears in a promotion for an online class in wine appreciation, it's likely he wants to do some good for his industry. Another reason, probably, is that he'd like some cash money for sharing his particular knowledge and expertise. (Fair enough. I wanted you to buy my book and you did. Thanks, by the way!)

But beyond Mr. Suckling's supposed financial motivations, I also have to assume that he's unearthed something more. I must believe he's discovered that understanding deepens appreciation. And that this is a secret worth giving away.

I'm fascinated by the old English word, understand. If you break it apart, you realize it means "to stand under." But apparently, it dates back to a time when "under" didn't mean "beneath" but "in the middle of" or "among."

To understand a wine, you've gotta get your nose into the glass. To understand a place, you need to stand in it, be a part of it. To understand a people, you must stand among them.

I am grateful that I have people in my life who appreciate me because they have put in the time to understand me. To stand with me. I've got friends who've wondered what it's been like to be a pastor's kid. Who've asked how going to a bazillion different schools impacted me. Who've checked in to see how my grief journey is going.

To arrive at such a place of understanding with another human being, to truly know them, takes time. It takes attention, energy, and devotion. It's an investment. There's a cost—to both understander and understandee. And yet "arrival" is probably not the right word to describe where we feel we end up. Do we ever truly achieve understanding? Isn't it something we are invited, continually, to seek?

When you talk to people who have been married for decades, it's not uncommon to hear them say things like, "My partner still surprises me." Which is great. Somewhere around the ten-year mark in my own marriage, someone told me that one of the best ways to nurture intimate relationship is to stay curious.

Stay curious.
Darn good advice.

The moment we think we've solved every riddle there is to another person, the spirit of enquiry that drew us to them begins to dissipate. And of course, the same thing happens if we just can't be bothered to learn anything more about them. Staying curious isn't only a marvellous way to nurture intimacy with a loved one. It's cogent counsel for health in all our relationships.

Could human flourishing depend on a commitment to curiosity? I wonder. And can we get there by asking each other questions besides "What do you do for a living?" Don't get me wrong. This question can and does lead to deeper conversations and greater levels of understanding and appreciation. Especially when it leads to common ground. We love it when we meet someone new and a shared interest comes up, and *bam,* there's a connection. *You're into Herbie Hancock, too? I had no idea!*

In my case, "What do you do for a living?" is a question that often serves to end a conversation, rather than open it further.

Well-Meaning Stranger: So, what do you do?
Me: I'm a pastor.
Stranger:

(If I had a nickel...)

Part of the problem, though, has to do with my unwillingness to answer the question with creativity. In a way that might lead the conversation in a different direction. Not to hide the truth of how I earn my livelihood, but to open the possibility for curiosity. Next time I'm asked this question, I'm going to try and muster the courage to say, "I try to practice the way of Jesus and encourage others to do the same."

It's possible that saying that may well shut things down even faster. But who knows? Perhaps it'll be a risk worth taking.

When I started my wine journey, one of the first things I learned was a simple approach to tasting wine. I learned it from Madeline Puckette (that witty wine expert and writer of Wine Folly I've mentioned a few times). Before I outline the method, I should say that it's not original to Puckette. It's used by pros all over the world. But this is close to the way Puckette describes.

There are four steps:

LOOK: A visual inspection of the wine under neutral lighting.

SMELL: Identify aromas through orthonasal olfaction (aka breathing through your nose).

TASTE: Assess both the taste structure (sour, bitter, sweet) and flavours derived from retronasal olfaction (aka breathing with the back of your nose). To do this, inhale as you take a sip and hold it in your mouth. Swish it around a bit with your tongue. This warms it up and releases the aromas. Swallow. Then exhale vigorously, with your mouth closed, through your nose. Taste that explosion of flavour and smell those aromas!

THINK/CONCLUDE: Develop a complete profile of a wine to store in your long-term memory.[2]

Over the years, I've practised this method to the point where my muscle memory is strong. My body naturally walks through the steps without the need to think about each one.

I get annoyed when the lighting at a winery tasting room *isn't* neutral or is too dim to see properly. There are times when I will take several minutes to just *look,* swirl, and sniff before even bringing the glass to my lips for a taste. "I could smell this all day," I say to anyone around, geeky as all-get-out. The aromas in a good wine often have a wooing effect on me. To say nothing of the taste.

I've got this crazy idea.

What if we were to apply something like this four-step wine tasting method to human interaction? Or at least the first three?

I don't want to push the metaphor too far here or make it too literal, because it just gets ridiculous if you do. I mean, am I saying you should walk up to a random human and take a good whiff? Nope. Hard pass.

Am I saying our goal should be to "develop a complete profile" of each person we meet? Should we treat them as suspects in a police investigation? Full interrogation and citizen's arrest a la Dwight Schrute? #Caseclosed? I am not.

And I fully realize that "visual inspection" can sound creepy, or airport security-esque. Or both.

Here's what I am saying:

LOOK

We need to remind ourselves to look at other humans.
To see them.

Eye contact is in short supply these days. Our default posture tends to avoid meeting peoples' gaze whenever possible. We're more often looking at screens, or into mirrors, or over the shoulders of the person right in front of us to *someone more important.*

Jesus' life was a master class in deep seeing.

> *Then he looked at those seated in a circle around him...*[3]

When he saw the crowds, he had compassion on them...[4]

The eye is the lamp of your body. When your eyes are healthy, your whole body also is full of light...[5]

What if we read the gospels through Jesus' deep-seeing lens? How might that change the way you see?

Here's an idea, for starters. The next time you're about to clink glasses with someone, look them in the eye. When you "cheers," convey that they matter. Use a few extra words if you have some. Pay attention to what happens in you as you do this. And if possible, notice what happens to those you see deeply.

Consider the phrase "under neutral lighting" with me. This is hugely important when looking at a glass of wine. You don't want to examine a red wine's appearance through pink neon glow. Like Cyndi Lauper, you want to see its true colours.

Might this notion of neutrality teach us something about how to hold and respect and honour peoples' stories? To look at a person under neutral lighting is to risk open-endedness. It means resisting the temptation to make assumptions and jump to conclusions. Your roots, your origins—your somewhereness—is not the same as theirs.

I think that far too often, we're threatened by difference. What would it look like, instead, to approach another's somewhereness with curiosity?

SMELL

You can look at someone from a distance and get a general sense of what they're like, but to truly get to know them—to build a (metaphorical) aromatic profile—you have to "smell" them. And to smell them, you need to get close. This is something you can't do at arm's length. A certain level of proximity is required.

TASTE

What if we were to see this step as an invitation to move even deeper into vulnerability? To get humble, honest, and open enough to move beyond closeness to actual contact. To dare to say, "I have touched that person's life, and their life has touched mine."

Again, I'm speaking metaphorically. I'm not talking about physical contact that disrespects personal boundaries. At the same time, we need to reclaim practices that encourage healthy and appropriate physical touch, even in the church.

In my church, we have worked hard to create environments for people to share their actual lives. For one life to touch another—to truly make a lasting *impression,* in the fullest sense of the word—more than Sunday services are needed.

We have small groups, called Neighbourhood Groups, that meet weekly in peoples' homes. They engage in four rhythms over the course of a month, which we call Directions.

The Withward Direction is about being with each other, regardless of what life is handing us. Upward is about being with God through Scripture, prayer, and spiritual practice. Outward is about being with and for our neighbours in tangible ways.

The tasting step is parallel to our Inward Direction, which is about:

moving past the surface of our lives
knowing and being known
practising vulnerability

THINK/CONCLUDE?

I'm not sure this one fits as well (metaphorically) as the other three. Should we *think* about each other? Of course. *Conclude,* though? I don't know. Sure, it works for Wine Club. You put pen to placemat and make your notes. You maybe even rate the wine on some sort of system. Conclude works if you're doing interviews for a job or auditions for a play. Your primary task is to make a conclusive decision about who gets the role and who doesn't. But in the realm of relationship, conclude feels too final, too judgmental. Still, we do it too often. I want to live more openly toward the people I meet.

Maybe the word understand can be of help here, in the way we explored it earlier. We seek to understand both wine and people by looking, smelling, tasting, and thinking. But it's never a conclusive process. It's always continuous.

Just as I don't have to like every single wine I taste, I don't have to like every human I encounter. But I am called to love them.

"Love one another," Jesus said. "This is how folks will know you're my apprentices."[6]

And to love someone, I need to try to connect with them:

To see them deeply.
To get close enough to appreciate each person's unique "aromas" (personality, habits, vibe).
To share life, to make impressions on each other.

Who knows, over a season of curiosity, I may even grow to like them. I may come to know that what knits us together is greater than what irks me about them or rubs me the wrong way. That we are not as separate as I once thought. I might even wake up one morning and realize I've made a new friend.

I've been looking for a more this-worldly spirituality.
The kind Jesus seemed to be on about. The One who said, *Consider the lilies.*

He said this in the middle of the best sermon he ever delivered.[7] In the original context, he was making a point about how you don't have to worry about your life: what you'll wear, what you'll eat, what you'll drink.

Basically, God's got you.

(This phrase may sound trite to our 21st- century ears. But, when you set it beside the other billion verses in Scripture that tell us to make sure *we've* got *each other,* the message is pretty darn clear. It's not one or the other. It's both.)

But to truly grasp this point—for the words to seep like water into the soil of our being, right down to the roots—we've got to get out in the field, find the lilies, and take a good look. It probably wouldn't hurt to smell them while we're there.

So we end where we began. Apprenticing at a winery not only helped me continue to grow my affection for wine. It's also helped me deepen my apprenticeship to the Jesus way. To the this-worldly spirituality he embodies. I truly hope it's helped you do the same.

Here then, dear reader, is what I want to leave you with as you close this book and pick up whatever else sits on your bedside table.

Consider the lilies.

Consider the details. Consider what's in front of you. And who's in front of you. Consider what's beneath the surface of your own life—the frantic paddling despite the calm exterior—and let that open you up to stay curious about what's going on for every fellow earthling who shares this glorious vineyard with us.

Consider your somewhereness.
Consider that of others.

Look.
Smell.
Taste.
Think.
Love.

Amen.

Gratitudes

I want to thank...

Terri, my wife—for believing I could write a book, and for giving yourself to this project in so many (mostly unseen) ways. Not least of which was being a solo parent when I was away writing, resting, or harvesting. Thanks for loving me well. I love you so much.

Adriana, my daughter—for being an unending source of wonder, and for teaching me at least as much as I teach you. I love you.

Pam and Chad Teigen—I don't know if this book would exist had you not moved up to wine country. You have not only helped nurture my wine enthusiasm. You've allowed our friendship to deepen and grow despite the distance. Big love to you both.

Richard Jones—for taking that lunch meeting with me when I first had the dream to do a wine apprenticeship during my sabbatical. And for believing in that dream enough to connect me to the industry folks who made it happen.

Arterra Wines Canada and the Nk'Mip Cellars staff team—for giving me opportunity to learn and work alongside you for a season. You are all such incredible, passionate, hospitable humans.

Volker and Elke Wagner—for your ongoing generosity in providing my family with a place to stay in Osoyoos.

Artisan Church, both its leadership and the wider community—for the gift of a sabbatical that led to this book being birthed. And for checking in and cheering me on along the way.

Blythe Kingcroft and Lance Odegard—for reading an early version of my manuscript and offering such valuable feedback. I'm so lucky to have such good friends who are also literary geniuses.

Danny Taylor—for your friendship, expertise, and invaluable assistance with Chapter Eight.

My Wine Club pals, past, present and future— for sharing my passion, not only for wine, but for life lived well. Your collective nerdery knows no bounds, and that fact will never cease to delight and inspire.

The SFD Club (*Shitty First Drafts,* a term coined by one of my writer heroes, Anne Lamott) —for getting together to read and critique each others' work. Although we didn't continue to meet, those sessions in the back room of The Main meant a lot to my first-time-author soul.

Steve Imbach, Lorie Martin, and Brent Unrau, my spiritual directors past and present, and to the entire SoulStream community—for deep friendship, partnership in, and commitment to the Christ-centred contemplative tradition. I wouldn't want to journey through life in any other way.

Dan and Sharon Williams—for lending me a beautiful place near the ocean to write for a few days, just as the world was ending.

The mighty coffee community in Vancouver—for faithfully providing several necessary accoutrements to the writing process: great coffee, friendly service, killer playlists, and dependable wifi.

My designer, Chelsea McKenzie—for making this book look more beautiful than I could have imagined.

My editor and longsuffering literary co-conspirator, Julia Kochuk—for making me a better writer, and a better person.

The True Vine—for abiding in me, as I abide in you.

Notes

INTRODUCTION

1 Psalm 8.

2 Psalm 72 is a good example of a prayer that links themes of creation and justice explicitly. I love how verse 3 is rendered in The Message: *Let the mountains give exuberant witness; shape the hills with the contours of right living.*

3 Matthew 13:34-35; Mark 4:33-34.

4 In several texts within the gospels, Jesus intentionally includes people who could be grouped in categories of last, least, lost, and little. Check out a few here: Matthew 20:16 (last); 25:40 (least); 18:11 (lost); 19:13-14 (little).

5 Wine for Normal People Podcast, https://www.winefornormalpeople.com/category/podcast/.

6 Jon Bonne, *The New Wine Rules* (New York: Ten Speed Press, 2017).

7 Sommelier at Home, https://www.sommathome.ca/.

CHAPTER ONE

1   There are, however, desert-like regions within the province. Not too many people know that in southwest Saskatchewan, there are 1900 square kilometres of sand dunes. Look up The Great Sandhills and be amazed!

2   Gerald Asher, *A Vineyard in My Glass* (Berkeley: University of California Press, 2011), back cover.

3   Asher, *A Vineyard in My Glass*, 2.

4   Asher, *A Vineyard in My Glass*, 84.

5   Roger Morris, "Does Terroir Matter?" *Wine Enthusiast*, November 13, 2018, https://www.winemag.com/2018/11/13/does-terroir-matter/.

6   Quoted in Huon Hooke, "Terroir: Reality or Fantasy," *The Real Review*, February 16, 2021, https://www.therealreview.com/2021/02/16/terroir-reality-or-fantasy/.

7   Matt Kramer, "What Makes Wine a Landmark," *Wine Spectator*, September 15, 1996, https://www.winespectator.com/articles/what-makes-a-wine-a-landmark-6873.

8   Does talk of Wine Club pique your interest? In a later chapter, I'm going to teach you how to start your own!

9   Alder Yarrow, "Tūrangawaewae: A Maori Expression of Terroir," *Vinography: A Wine Blog*, February 2, 2017, https://www.vinography.com/2017/02/turangawhaewhae_a_maori_expres.

CHAPTER TWO

1   Terry Theise, *What Makes a Wine Worth Drinking* (New York: Houghton Mifflin Harcourt, 2018), 59.

2   Theise, *What Makes a Wine*, 59.

3   Arterra farms a total of nearly 1300 acres of Okanagan vineyards.

4   To be clear, "Vineyard Boss Nelson" is my nickname for him, not his. Also using it to set us two Nelsons apart. It was feeling a little crowded.

5   I'll introduce Picton, as well as the rest of the Nk'Mip winemaking team, more fully in Chapter 5.

6   Once a star in the Jackson-Triggs portfolio, in 2019 Sunrock Vineyards became its own single vineyard red wine brand (still within Arterra). If you like a big, bold, spicy Shiraz, Sunrock is good value for the money.

7   John 15:1-2.

8   John 15:4.

9   John 15:5.

10 When I think of the word pastoral in this agrarian sense, what immediately comes to mind are the opening movements of Beethoven's Sixth Symphony. As one of only two symphonies that Beethoven specifically named, he called it "Pastoral Symphony, or Recollections of Country Life." It was composed with "extra-musical" purpose—as an expression of nature, complete with creek ripples and bird calls.

CHAPTER THREE

1   Jay McInerney, "Wine Country: Is Canada the New Napa?" *Town & Country*, February 2, 2020, https://www.townandcountrymag.com/leisure/drinks/a30316108/canada-new-napa/.

2   McInerney, "Wine Country"

3   What's the difference between a viticulturist and a vineyard manager? A viticulturist specializes in the culture or cultivation of grapes, especially for winemaking. A viticulturist may be involved in research and teaching, as well as breeding, developing, and evaluating new varieties of grapes. A vineyard manager manages the land and the vines producing the grape crop used to make wine. In my case, there seemed to be a lot of overlap between the two roles. Both Mike Watson (viticulturist) and Nelson Dutra (vineyard manager) were directly involved with farmers and vineyard workers. And both used their skills and expertise to assist in the maintenance of healthy vineyards to make the best possible wine.

4   Vij's Books, https://vijs.ca/books/.

5   Kevin Espiritu, "Cutworms: How To Destroy Noctuidae Caterpillars In Your Garden," *Epic Gardening*, June 14, 2019, https://www.epicgardening.com/cutworms/.

6   Maia Szalavitz, "Touching Empathy," *Psychology Today*, March 1, 2010, https://www.psychologytoday.com/us/blog/born-love/201003/touching-empathy.

7   Matthew 13:24-30.

8   Matthew 13:29-30.

9   Richard Rohr, "The Weeds and the Wheat," *Center for Action and Contemplation*, December 5, 2016, https://cac.org/weeds-and-wheat-2016-12-05/.

CHAPTER FOUR

1   Varietal = type of grape.

2   Jim Duane, "Working a First Harvest: Ben Matthews and Cameron Laurent," *Inside Winemaking Podcast*, Episode 83, https://www.insidewinemaking.com/#/083/.

3   Aaron Crey is currently the Consulting Winemaker and Partner at Vintner's Cove Winery (Okanagan, BC).

4   Racking means moving wine from one vessel to another: from tank to barrel, barrel to barrel, barrel to tank.

5   Madeline Puckette, "How Wine Making Processes Affect Wine," *Wine Folly*, January 27, 2014, https://winefolly.com/deep-dive/wine-making-processes-affect-wines-flavor/.

6   Zadie Smith, "Peonies," in *Intimations: Six Essays* (London: Penguin Books, 2020), 7.

7   As writer and podcaster Nora McInerny put it in her TED Talk from 2019, "We don't 'move on' from grief, we move forward with it."

8   I love what womanist theologian Dr. Wil Gafney said in an interview in Waco, Texas: "Job remains my favorite book; I keep coming back to it. I like Job because its honesty about the inscrutability of God and suffering reflects how I understand the world. It grants permission to argue with and protest to God about things that are not right." I think we need to be more honest about naming suffering that is senseless and tragic. Interview available: https://eewc.com/an-interview-with-dr-wil-gafney/.

9   Colossians 1:19-20.

10 Hebrews 12:1-3 (MSG).

11 John 16:33.

12 Ruth Haley Barton, "Fall Garden," *Transforming Center*, 2012, https://transformingcenter.org/2017/11/fall-garden/.

CHAPTER FIVE

1 https://www.vintnerscovewinery.ca/.

2 Google "supertaster" if you're curious, or if you think you might be one.

3 Max Coane, in "The Everything Guide to Brettanomyces," *SevenFiftyDaily*, April 25, 2018, https://daily.sevenfifty.com/the-everything-guide-to-brettanomyces/.

4 2 Corinthians 5:7.

5 Thomas Keating, *Invitation to Love* (London: Bloomsbury Academic, 20th Anniversary ed., 2012), 139-40. Square brackets contain my definition of contemplative practice which, while influenced by Keating, is not a direct quote.

6 Scott Erickson, *Honest Advent* (Grand Rapids: Zondervan, 2020), 85-86.

CHAPTER SIX

1 Plus, a good chunk of 2021, and who knows how much longer? Lord have mercy.

2 Dr. Vinny, "Where does the extra wine come from for 'topping off' a barrel?" *Wine Spectator,* January 19, 2015, https://www.winespectator.com/articles/where-does-the-extra-wine-come-from-for-topping-off-a-barrel-51121.

CHAPTER SEVEN

1 ROFL is an abbreviation commonly used in text-speak. It stands for Rolling On the Floor Laughing.

2   Terry Theise, *Reading Between the Wines* (Berkeley: University of California Press, 2010), 78.

3   Scott Erickson, image available: https://www.instagram.com/p/B1WfAV8gRDL/.

4   Barry and Connolly, *The Practice of Spiritual Direction* (San Francisco: HarperOne, 2nd ed, 2009), 53. Content in square brackets is mine.

5   Barry and Connolly, *The Practice of Spiritual Direction*, 54.

6   Rocca delle Macìe is one of my Chianti Classico go-tos. They produce wine of consistent quality that's also relatively inexpensive—around $20 CAD.

CHAPTER EIGHT

1   Gisela H. Kreglinger, *The Spirituality of Wine* (Grand Rapids: Wm. B. Eerdmans, 2016), 181.

2   Kreglinger, *The Spirituality of Wine*, 181.

3   A German noun meaning "alcohol", or "spirits of wine".

4   This article, which my friend Danny Taylor pointed me towards, is super helpful in explaining how the language we use regarding addiction matters a great deal: https://www.naabt.org/documents/naabt_language.pdf.

5   See Genesis 9:20-26.

6   You can read that super fun story in Genesis 19:30-38. Patriarchal interpretations of this text (and indeed, the plain/literal reading of it) often seem to indicate that the daughters were to blame for getting their father drunk and seducing him. Womanist readings of Genesis 19, however, give us solid, well-researched reasons to believe otherwise. See, for example, Wil Gafney's work here: https://www.wilgafney.com/2017/03/12/smashing-the-biblical-patriarchy/. Or consider this article by Dr. Ilan Kutz, one of Israel's leading psychiatrists in the field of post-trauma, writing at the intersection of biblical theology and science: https://www.ncbi.nlm.nih.gov/pmc/articles/PMC1322245/. In this author's opinion, these interpretations are worth paying attention to.

7   2 Samuel 11.

8   Brian McLaren, in Nathan Frambach, *Emerging Ministry: Being*

Church Today (Minneapolis: Augsburg Books, 2007), 49.

9   Psalm 30:5 (MSG).

10 Deuteronomy 7:13, 14:26; Psalm 104:14-15; Ecclesiastes 9:7; Isaiah
    25:6, 55:1; Joel 3:18; Amos 9:13-14; John 2:1-11; 1 Timothy 5:23 (wine
    as medicine!)

11 Kreglinger, *The Spirituality of Wine*, 183.

12 Isaiah 5:11-12.

13 Brené Brown, *Dare to Lead: Brave Work. Tough Conversations.
    Whole Hearts.* (New York: Random House, 2018), 84.

14 Danny Taylor, MC, RCC, personal conversation.

15 Taylor, personal conversation.

16 Brown, *Dare to Lead*, 85.

CHAPTER NINE

1   If the Enneagram is unfamiliar to you, shame on you for skipping
    Chapter 2. Just kidding. This book is a no-shame zone. But hop on
    back there for a very short primer.

2   Charlie Mackesy, *The Boy, the Mole, the Fox and the Horse* (San
    Francisco: HarperOne, 2019). I'd gladly give a page number, but
    there aren't any in the hardcover version I have. This scene is
    about two-thirds through the book, on the left-hand side.

3   Madeline Puckette, "Wine Tasting Placemats," *Wine Folly*, updat-
    ed March 23, 2021, https://winefolly.com/tips/wine-placemats/.

4   Madeline Puckette, "Updated Wine Flavor Wheel with 100+
    Flavors," *Wine Folly,* updated August 25, 2020, https://winefolly.
    com/tips/wine-aroma-wheel-100-flavors/.

5   What a lot of folks don't know is that Champagne is a region in
    France, not a term for all wine that has bubbles. Another fun fact:
    unless your sparkling wine is actually produced in Champagne,
    you can't legally call it Champagne.

6   In Ethan Fixell, "4 Master Sommeliers on the Reality of the Job
    Today," *Food & Wine*, updated May 24, 2017, https://www.foodan-
    dwine.com/wine/4-master-sommeliers-reality-job-today.

7   Psalm 1:1-3.

8   Psalm 8:3-4.

9   Psalm 18:1-2 (MSG).

10   Psalm 34:8.

CHAPTER TEN

1   https://www.youtube.com/watch?v=GHqdrPYys9c.

2   Brother Roger, *Opening Paths of Trust* (Taizé: Ateliers at Presses de Taizé, 2003). No page numbers, as it's more brochure than book.

3   Author unknown, "The Value of Silence," Taizé website, https://www.taize.fr/en_article12.html

4   Author unknown, "The Value of Silence"

5   Joan Vander Vliet, an active member of the Second Congregational Church of Greenfield (New England), said this of the silence of Taizé. Available: https://www.sneucc.org/newsdetail/95853.

6   Matt Kramer, *Matt Kramer On Wine* (New York: Sterling Epicure, 2010), 253.

7   Kramer, *Matt Kramer On Wine*, 253.

8   Kramer, *Matt Kramer On Wine*, 253.

9   Kramer, *Matt Kramer On Wine*, 253.

10   Jane Anson, "Why a Decline in Soil Health Should Worry All Wine Lovers," *Decanter*, December 4, 2017, https://www.decanter.com/wine-news/opinion/news-blogs-anson/wine-and-soil-health-bourguignon-352159/.

11   Anson, "Why a Decline".

12   Claude and Lydia Bourguignon, "Claude and Lydia Bourguignon," Available: https://www.dahu.bio/en/knowledge/agriculture/claude-and-lydia-bourguignon. Also, did you know that 80% of life on earth is in the soil? According to the Bourguignons, the mass of earthworms on the planet is greater than the mass of all the other animals combined. (Mind. Blown.)

13   Bourguignon, "Claude and Lydia."

14   Matthew 6:28; Luke 12:27. Jesus learned well from the psalmeliers! (See Chapter 9.)

15   Ecclesiastes 3:1-2a, 8 (NIV).

16   Basso Services Viticoles on Instagram. Available: https://www.instagram.com/p/B_IOqq0JFuM/?utm_source=ig_web_copy_link.

17 Richard Rohr, *Everything Belongs: The Gift of Contemplative Prayer* (Pearl River: Crossroad Publishing, 2003), 73-74.

18 Rohr, *Everything Belongs*, 74.

19 Rohr, *Everything Belongs*, 75.

20 The Nap Ministry on Instagram. Available: https://www.instagram.com/thenapministry/.

CHAPTER ELEVEN

1 France's classification systems can be confusing. Partly because they're not standardized across the country. The designations differ from region to region. For example, in Burgundy, Grand Cru (cru means "growth") is top dog, whereas Premier Cru is the next highest. In Bordeaux, it's reversed. Premier Cru is the highest, followed by Grand Cru.

2 See Chapter 9 (the wine club stuff) for more detail on developing a profile using a tasting placemat and other resources.

3 Mark 3:34.

4 Matthew 9:36.

5 Matthew 6:22.

6 John 13:34-35 (my paraphrase).

7 The "Sermon on the Mount," in Matthew 5-7, is widely regarded by scholars as a distillation of Jesus' best teaching.

The Author

NELSON BOSCHMAN

Nelson Boschman is a pastor, writer, spiritual director, jazz musician, wine enthusiast, husband, and father of one in Vancouver, British Columbia. He is the pastor of spiritual formation at Artisan Church, and a partner of SoulStream.org, a community that seeks to nurture contemplative experience with Christ, leading to inner freedom and loving service. Connect with him at *NelsonBoschman.com* and follow him on Instagram *@nelsonboschman*.

www.NelsonBoschman.com

Photo: Britney Berrner

Colophon

What's this now, you ask? A Colophon. The Greek origin of the word means "finishing stroke" or "final touch." It's a break of the fourth wall, a move from the book's content to the design of the words themselves.

Super Meta.
A terroir of type.

The cover holds characters of different sizes and cases, evocative of turn-of-the-last-century poster design: type only. At the printing press back in the day, hot metal letters were used by the tray-full. On occasion, a typesetter would run out of *just the right piece*. When that happened, they'd say, "I'm out of sorts." The printer had to improvise with what remained. The varied sizes of letters in the word *Growing* reminds us to playfully notice the whole and the parts simultaneously, kinda like wine. The letters seem to grow out of each other.

Do you see a hanging cluster of grapes?
Ha. You can't unsee it now.
You're welcome.

The display typeface is **Voyage**. The letterforms are evocative of a quirky traveler who is strong, yet has stylish sensibilities. It's designed by VJ-Type, an independent type foundry based in Paris, France, known for distinctive fonts. The romantic confidence in this statuesque serif fills the cover and chapters sections with an Old World elegance.

The body text, set at 11pt/14pt, is *Minion Variable Concept*—used in regular, italic, and bold. Robert Slimbach of Adobe designed this font in the 1990's as an update to late Renaissance-era type for extended reading.

Block titles are set in **Grotesque MT Std**—a riff on the Monotype Grotesque typeface—with shapes updated from typographer Berthold's Ideal Grotesque, which is widely regarded as one of the great sans serifs.

Finally **Space Mono**, used only on the cover, feels like a type-writter in space, representing the New World. Even in fonts, there's always room to grow.

Illustrations in this edition are scanned from archival woodcut drawings about the creation and making of wine.